ALSO BY J. BRYAN, III

HODGEPODGE TWO

J. Bryan, III

HODGEPODGE TWO

ANOTHER COMMONPLACE BOOK

New York

ATHENEUM

1989

Atheneum
Macmillan Publishing Company
866 Third Avenue, New York, N.Y. 10022
Collier Macmillan Canada, Inc.

Library of Congress Cataloging-in-Publication Data
Bryan, J. (Joseph), 1904–
Hodgepodge Two : another commonplace book / J. Bryan, III.
p.   cm.
ISBN 0-689-12064-8
1. Commonplace-books.   I. Title.
PN6245.B844   1989
818'.5203—dc19   89-6513   CIP

Macmillan books are available at special discounts for bulk purchases
for sales promotions, premiums, fund-raising, or educational use.
For details, contact:

Special Sales Director
Macmillan Publishing Company
866 Third Avenue
New York, N.Y. 10022

10 9 8 7 6 5 4 3 2 1

Printed in the United States of America

For
my great-aunt
Annie Carter Stewart
1853–1957
with love and admiration

[Sherlock Holmes remarked,] I am an omnivorous reader, with an extremely retentive memory for trifles.

SIR ARTHUR CONAN DOYLE
"The Adventure of the Lion's Mane"

I look upon anecdotes as debts due to the public, which every man, when he has that kind of cash by him, ought to pay.

LORD ORRERY

Foreword

No sooner had the first *Hodgepodge* gone on sale than fresh items began coming to mind and hand—so abundantly, indeed, that they have encouraged me to etc., etc. What follows is the pick of the collection; some are my own, others were sent in by readers. If my filing system weren't so primitive, every item hereinafter would be credited to its proper source. As it is, I have given credit only where my leaky memory permitted. My most generous contributors include the following:

E. J. Applewhite, C. D. B. Bryan, Todd Culbertson, Rosemary Dyer, Clifton Fadiman, Joan Gates, the late George D. Gibson, Tommy Grymes, Katherine Hamilton, James Jackson Kilpatrick, Elizabeth Longford, James McCargar, Dr. Thomas Murrell, Pinkney Near, Mark Norman, Dick Perkins, Glenn Perry, Thomas Pinckney, Willis Player, Parke Rouse, Jr., William S. Simpson, Jr. (and the staffs of the Richmond Public Libraries), William M. Spackman, the late Chauncey Stillman, Caskie Stinnett, Dr. Richard D. Wilson, and Bob Wrenn.

I make special, gold-star mention of three others: John R. Cournyer, who sent me (among a dozen other items) the single most extraordinary one (I think) in this book: the Shakespeare-Bible coincidence on page 32. William S. Sims, Jr., deserves a credit line on almost every page, so generous and interesting have been his contributions. Lastly, and preeminently, I acknowledge my debt to Norman Hickman. Sherlock Holmes said of his brother Mycroft, "Other men have one specialty, but his specialty is omniscience." Holmes might have been speaking of Norman Hickman. Himself the author-compiler of three fascinating quiz books, he made his surplus available to me, and I have drawn upon it without stint. The surprising item about the foundation of the British Empire (page 214) is a typical Hickman tidbit. To him and to the other contributors I have listed, I frankly, freely, and gratefully declare my debt.

J. Bryan, III

Brook Hill,
Richmond, Virginia 23227

Just as this book went to press, I received the grievous news of Norman Hickman's death.

Contents

---

*Whenever a chapter title is followed by "(Cont'd),"
as here, it means that the category is an amplification
of one that first appeared in *Hodgepodge*.

Contents

Contents

Contents

HODGEPODGE TWO

Absent-mindedness
(CONT'D)

GENERAL YOANNES METAXAS, the dictator of Greece from 1936 to 1941, was notoriously absent-minded. Once, as a passenger in a military seaplane, he asked the pilot if he might fly it for a while. They changed places and in the course of time, Metaxas prepared to land at an airport.

"Sir," the pilot said nervously, "this is a *seaplane!*"

"Of course! Of course!" Metaxas said, and swung out over the bay where he brought the plane down safely. He thanked the pilot, opened the door of the cabin, and stepped out into the sea.

JOHN R. COURNYER

Carolus Clusis, who wrote the first monograph on tulips (1567), was so absent-minded that he once signed a letter with the name of a friend.

1

Patient: "I can't think what's the matter with me, Doctor. I can't remember a thing!"

Doctor: "Dear, dear! When did this start?"

Patient: "When did *what* start?"

I recently turned 50 . . . and I am having to learn to accept a new me; one who dials a telephone number and, while the 'phone is ringing, forgets whom he is calling.

BILL COSBY, *Time Flies*

Canon W. A. Spooner of New College, Oxford, was celebrated not only for his "Spoonerisms"—e.g., "Mardon me, Padam, you are occupewing my pie. May I sew you to another sheet?" but for his absent-mindedness. Once at a dinner he spilled some salt on the tablecloth, but immediately set things right by picking up the decanter of claret and pouring it over the spill.

The Royal Navy likes to remember the celebrated vice admiral who died full of years and honors. When his strongbox was opened, a card inside it met the eyes of his executors:

Starboard—RIGHT
Port—LEFT

Captain Frank Winston, of Louisa Courthouse, Virginia, had walked the few hundred yards from his house to the railroad depot when he suddenly felt his coat pocket and exclaimed, "I do declare, I believe I've left my watch at home! I wonder if I have time to go back and fetch it?" So saying, he took his watch from his trousers pocket and saw it was still fifteen minutes to train-time. "Yes, yes," he said, "plenty of time," and turned back home.

Actors and Actresses
(CONT'D)

ALL ACTORS have methods. Ethel Merman's was to work to the audience, rather than to the other actors. This enabled her to drive perfectly good leading men to the hospital.

GEORGE ABBOTT

Method acting? There are quite a few methods. Mine involves a lot of talent, a glass and some cracked ice.

JOHN BARRYMORE

Roberto Rossellini: "All Italians are good actors."
Orson Welles: "The only bad ones are on the stage and screen."

At the rehearsal of his daughter Cornelia's wedding, the actor Otis Skinner asked the minister how he should answer when asked, "Who giveth this woman?"

4

The minister said, "You don't answer. You just hand her over."

"Nonsense!" Skinner cried. "I've never played a walk-on part in all my life!"

In Hollywood, a "starlet" is the name for any woman under thirty who is not actively employed in a brothel.

BEN HECHT

Although Katharine Hepburn was once labeled "box-office poison," she is the only performer to have won four Oscars.

When Spencer Tracy was chided for demanding top billing over her, and was reminded of the traditional "Ladies first!" he protested, "This is a movie, not a lifeboat."

Warner Brothers, who produced *Casablanca*, tried to sue the Marx Brothers for naming their film *A Night in Casablanca*. Groucho put a stop to that nonsense by threatening to sue Warners for plagiarizing the name "Brothers."

Some of the greatest love affairs I've known have involved one actor, unassisted.

WILSON MIZNER

The Theatre Guild was casting a new drama. One actor gave such a brilliant reading that the director told him, "I don't need to hear anyone else read for 'Captain Dalton.' The role is yours. What is your name please?"

"Thank you," the actor said. "My name is Ernest Armpit."

"I beg your pardon?"

"Ernest Armpit."

The director seemed to struggle with a strong emotion. At last he managed to say, "Mr. Armpit, this is the Theatre Guild. We are an organization of distinction and propriety. You cannot expect us to print a program announcing that Captain Dalton is played by an Ernest Armpit. That is simply out of the question. I'm sorry, but you'll have to take a stage name."

The actor drew himself up, lifted his chin, and glared down his nose. "Sir," he said coldly, "that *is* my stage name."

ELAINE STEINBACK

An actor is something less than a man, while an actress is something more than a woman.

RICHARD BURTON

I'm afraid you'll never make it as an actor. But as a star, I think you might well hit the jackpot.

ORSON WELLES, to Joseph Cotten

Nostalgia

Raymond Hitchcock ... the Duncan Sisters ... Jack Holt ... Fatty Arbuckle ... Al St. John ... Kala Pasha ... Mack Swain ... Louise Fazenda ... Mabel Norman ... Richard Barthelmess ... Lionel, Ethel, and Jack ... Ronald Colman ... Bessie Barriscale ... Thomas Meighan ... William and Dustin Farnum ... Mary Miles Minter ... Marguerite Clark ... John Bunny ... Yale Boss ... Lew Cody ... Rin Tin Tin ... Wallace Reid ... Bobby Vernon ... Mae Marsh ... Valeska Suratt ... Alla Nazimova ... Theda Bara ... Barbara Lamarr ... Norma Shearer ... Constance and Norma Talmadge ... Gaby Delys ... Corinne Griffith ... Frank Tinney ... Ray Dooley ... George Arliss ... the Floradora Sextette ... Harry Lauder ... Leon Errol ... Lenore Ulrich ... Tallulah Bankhead ... Frank Morgan ... Katherine Cornell ... Alfred Lunt ... Lynn Fontanne ... Louis Tellegan ... Jeanne Eagles ... Ina Claire ...

Told by the late Tam Williams, an English actor:
"Several times I had the privilege of acting with Stella [Mrs. Pat Campbell]. One performance I shall never forget. She stopped it cold, right in midscene, and ordered me to go to her dressing room and fetch her shawl. I left. The other actors waited. The audience waited. I reentered with the shawl and put it around Stella's shoulders, and the play resumed."

Edith Wheeler, a veteran actress, was playing the death scene in a Baltimore production of *The Drunkard*, in November 1986, when she dropped to the stage and, to tremendous applause, died.

6

"She told me she's an actress. What sort of things does she act in?"

"Mostly in old-fashioned settings with four posts."

CARL VAN VECHTEN

The most famous of the Lone Rangers, Earle Graser, was never west of Detroit (the home station of the series) in his life. Nor was anyone else in the cast except Tonto, who had been to Colorado once, with a Klaw & Erlanger road show.

Airplanes and Rockets

A WOMAN TELEPHONED the New York office of British Airways and asked how long was the Concorde flight between New York and London. The agent said, "Just a minute," and went to look up the schedule. When he returned, the caller had hung up, apparently satisfied.

The world's first jet-engine aircraft, a Heinkel He-178, piloted by Erich Warsitz, took to the air over Germany on August 27, 1939. In the course of the test flight, Warsitz hit a bird and made a forced landing. The first jet-engine pilot thus became also the first to suffer jet engine failure because of a bird.

Advice to air passengers:
Don't drink; it slows the reflexes if you have to escape. Wear multiple layers of light-colored natural fabrics, like cotton or

wool. Avoid synthetic materials; they melt in a fire. The worst thing you can wear is leather.

GREG JARRELLS, consultant to the Aviation Institute

A modern fighter pilot, suited up and hung with all his trappings, weighs more than a medieval knight in full armor.

When air pressure clogs your ears, don't hold your nose and blow. It might drive infection into your ears. Instead, make yourself yawn.

The *Enola Gay*, which dropped the Bomb on Hiroshima, was named for the pilot's mother. We also probably recognize the *Spirit of St. Louis* and the *Voyager*. But what was the name of the Wright brothers' first plane? Answer: *Flyer*.

What Orville Wright achieved on December 17, 1903, was the world's first successful, controlled, powered, manned, heavier-than-air flight. All these qualifiers are important.

Flyer weighed less than the nose-gear alone of a Boeing 707, America's first commercial jet, and *Flyer*'s first flight, 127 feet, was 8 feet shorter than the 707's wingspan.

Howard Hughes's H-4 flying boat, dubbed the *Spruce Goose*, with eight engines and a wingspan of 320 feet, was the largest plane ever built. Despite its size (or perhaps because of it), its longest flight was about a mile, at an altitude of only 70 feet. It is now "in mothballs" at Long Beach, California.

In the early 1900s, Alberto Santos-Dumont, a rich, Brazil-born pioneer in the construction and flying of dirigibles, was one of the sights of Paris. John Toland writes, "It was not uncommon to see his airship sail down the rue Washington and hover over his ornate apartment until a butler, standing on the steps, would haul him down."

Henry Luce of *Time-Life-Fortune* enjoyed challenging his guests with questions on arcane subjects. One night at dinner, he suddenly demanded, "Whatever became of Santos-Dumont?" Someone volunteered, "He died when his dirigible broke in two over Rio de Janeiro."

Archie MacLeish shrugged. "What else could you expect of a man with a hyphenated name?"

Actually, Santos-Dumont became so distressed by the use of dirigibles to drop bombs on civilians in the Great War that he committed suicide.

All right: We remember *The Spirit of St. Louis*, the *Enola Gay*, the *Flyer*, the *Spruce Goose*, the *Voyager* and a few others, but what about *Tingmissartoq*? The name is Eskimo for "the man who flies like a big bird." You should now recognize it as the plane in which Charles and Anne Lindbergh made two major flights, to the Arctic and the Orient.

The term "mach" as a measure of speed commemorates the German physicist Ernst Mach.

The Alphabet

THE MALTESE ALPHABET includes a letter H with a double crossbar and a Q with a dot over it.

R is called the *littera canina* in Latin, because it is thought to sound like a dog snarling.

The letters A, M, T, U, V, and W are symmetrical vertically; B, C, D, and K are symmetrical horizontally; H, I, O and X are symmetrical both ways.

In the 1890s Sir Henry d'Avigdor-Goldsmid laid out the entire park at Rendcome in the form of the letters of the Hebrew alphabet.

HUGH VICKERS and CAROLINE MCCULLOUGH,
Great Country Houses

The newest letter in the alphabet is J. Swedes find it difficult to pronounce, as witness the old song that begins:

> My name is Yon Yonson
> I come from Visconsin.

The Chinese have trouble with R, and the Japanese with L. During the Solomons campaign in World War II, their troops used to yell over their loudspeakers, "To herr with Babe Ruth!" Somehow it failed to strike terror into American hearts.

The Polynesian alphabet consists of only twelve letters: A, E, H, I, K, L, M, N, O, P, U, W.

The five vowels appearing on the tomb of Emperor Friedrich III of Austria (1415–93) in St. Stephen's Church, Vienna, are the initials of the words of his motto in two languages: In German, *A*lles *E*rdreich *I*st *Ö*sterreich *U*ntertan; in Latin, *A*ustriae *E*st *I*mperare *O*rbi *U*niverso. Both have the same meaning; loosely, "Austria rules the whole world."

The shortest English sentence that contains all the letters of the alphabet is: "QUICK WAFTING ZEPHYRS VEX BOLD JIM."

C. C. BOMBAUGH,
Oddities and Curiosities of Words and Literature

This is thirty letters, but Bill Sims has come up with one of only twenty-nine: BLOWZY FRUMPS HAD QUIT VEXING JACK.

In 1939, Ernest V. Wright published a 50,000 word novel, *Gadsby*, in which the letter E never appeared.

U is a nice old letter. It's simple to form (like I and X), easy to pronounce (unlike H and W), equipped with homonyms (you, ewe) that invite mild puns, and—upside down—handy for traffic signs and croquet courts. More's the pity, then, that Q, so long and so often U's companion, seems to be breaking off their alliance. The news from the Near East has accustomed us to such grotesqueries as Qabatiya (Jordan), Qanayah (Syria), and Qafi (Yemen); and if the Chinese insist on last names like Qiping and Qinghe, well, that's their own inscrutable business. But *must* DuPont call its new fabric "Qiana"? Don't let our U's fall into desuetude! Restore them to full use! "No U's is bad news."

S looks like a snake and sounds like a snake. Fear of snakes is worldwide, and the hissing snake sounds—*psst*! and *shh*!—mean "Look out!" or "Quiet!" in almost all languages. It is significant that the Hawaiian alphabet includes no S. Nor are there snakes in Hawaii or, for that matter, throughout nearly the whole of Polynesia.

ROSEMARY DYER

Z is the only letter with three pronunciations: *zee, zed,* and among certain old-fashioned, back-country Southerners, *izzard*—which survives chiefly in the phrase, "from Az to Izzard."

IB.

It has been a century since the word "Kodak" was registered by George Eastman as his trademark. . . . "The letter K has been a favorite with me," Eastman once explained, when asked how he had coined the name: "It seems a strong, incisive letter. It became a question of trying out a great number of combinations of letters that made words starting and ending with 'K.' The word 'Kodak' was the result."

American History Illustrated, September 1988

K may have been "strong and incisive" to Mr. Eastman, but there is still something inherently comic about it. Consider the "joke towns" once beloved of vaudeville comedians: Keokuk, Yonkers, Brooklyn, Hoboken, Kalamazoo, Skaneateles, Kankakee, Podunk. Dubuque belongs on this list; it has no K, but it has the K sound. And I remember a song that was popular in Honolulu some years ago: "The Cock-Eyed Mayor of Kaunakanai."

America, to British Eyes and Ears

A RICHMOND LADY, née Campbell, is proud of her Scots ancestry and keeps in touch with her clanfolk North of the Border. One of them notified her that he was planning his first trip to the States, and would like to pay his respects. She was delighted. The date and time of his arrival in Richmond were fixed; she would meet him at the airport, but how would she recognize him?

"Not to worry, Cousin," he wrote back. "Forbye I'll be the only man there wearing a kilt in the Campbell tartan."

Americans have no conversation. They only relate anecdotes.
An Englishman

Your women shall scream like peacocks when they talk, and your men neigh like horses when they laugh.
RUDYARD KIPLING

15

I am willing to love all mankind, except an American.

DR. SAMUEL JOHNSON

Art and Artists
(CONT'D)

ART IS POETRY without words.

HORACE

The Viennese artist who designed a poster for "Teddy's Perspiration Powder" shortly before the Great War, later gave up art for another line of work and became well known as A. Hitler.

"There are only two styles of portrait painting: the serious and the smirk."

CHARLES DICKENS, *Nicholas Nickleby*, Miss La Creevy speaking

Beware of artistic protestation: the real artist does not wear a red waistcoat and is not eager to talk of himself.

ANDRÉ GIDE, Journals

Al Hirschfeld, one of whose brilliant caricatures appears almost every Sunday in the "Arts and Leisure" section of the *New*

17

York Times, can draw in the dark. He can also draw in his pocket. Alva Johnston, the great *Times* reporter, could take notes in his pocket. He learned the trick when he realized that the sight of a notebook and pencil made some interviewees nervous.

If I spit, they will take my spit and frame it as great art.

PABLO PICASSO

The butterfly that Whistler signed to his paintings and etchings is probably the most familiar of artists' logos, but there are many others. They go back to the fourteenth century, when we find Jean Pucelle of France signing his paintings with a dragonfly. Lucas Cranach of Germany (1472–1553) signed with a dragon, its wings folded.

Henri met de Bles, Flemish (sixteenth century) used an owl. George Hoofnagel, also a sixteenth-century Flamand, used a nail. (*Nagel* is the German for "nail.") Judith Lyster, Dutch, seventeenth century, signed a lodestar, *leyster*, in Dutch. Edward Troye, a nineteenth-century American who specialized in painting Thoroughbred horses, liked to put a small shrub or bush in a lower corner of his canvases. Walter Crance, English (1845–1915), used the silhouette of a crane standing on one leg. Paul Klee, a Swiss (1879–1940), signed with a clover, *Klee* in German. He painted and drew with his left hand and wrote with his right. (President James Madison wrote equally well with either

18

hand.) Jean Cocteau, of France (1889–1962?), signed with a lop-sided star. And Fritz Hundertwasser, an Austrian, born in 1928, signed with the figure "100" followed by some waves.

Abstract art: A product of the unlettered sold by the unprin-cipled to the utterly bewildered.

AL CAPP

If you are puzzled by Jean Dubuffet's art, you have reason to be. He sought his inspiration in *graffiti* and in drawings by chil-dren, primitive people, and mental patients.

He is an artist, but he will always be hampered by thinking he sees what he has been brought up to think he sees.

MARY E. WILKINS FREEMAN, The Holte Family

After visiting the first exhibition of the European avant-garde artists, in 1913, James A. Stillman, the New York banker, ob-served, "Something is wrong with the world. These men know."

There is a great deal to be said for the Arts. For one thing, they offer the only career in which commercial failure is not necessarily discreditable.

EVELYN WAUGH

I was once taken to the Montmartre studio of a famous French painter. It was on the fifth floor, and as we climbed the creaking stairs, my escort told me this story:

Monsieur X, here, was one of the outstanding heroes of the French Resistance. When the war was over, De Gaulle sent for him and asked how the Fatherland could show its gratitude for his help. "There is no medal precious enough to represent your magnificent performance, but surely I can do something else for you? You have only to name it."

Here we reached the top floor, and my escort knocked on a door, then resumed, "Monsieur X said, 'Yes, general, there is one thing I would like: official permission to spend the rest of my life as a woman.'"

The door was opened by a man. "Madame is expecting you,"

19

he said. "Madame" came forward. "She" was wearing a chic black dress, and her red hair was neatly coiffed . . .

What garlic is to a salad, insanity is to art.

AUGUSTUS SAINT-GAUDENS

There is only one difference between a madman and me. I am not mad.

SALVADOR DALI

We visited the National Gallery of Art, with its remarkable collection of hand-painted pictures; and I can still recall the delicacy with which my father would intervene to shelter me from any that contained an undraped female figure.

*Augustus Carp, Esq. by Himself**

Norman Rockwell's "Four Freedoms" paintings are the most widely distributed paintings in history; tens of millions were sent all over the world in World War II. For paint rags he used diapers, buying them in fifty-dollar lots.

BERNIE SMITH, *The Joy of Trivia*

I don't know why it is that French artists lend their names so readily to puns, but they do. The first I ever heard was Charles Poore's superb "More in Seurat than in Ingres." Then Edward Lyttelton came along with "Arise! You have nothing Toulouse but Lautrec." Abel Green, the late editor of *Variety*, joined with Finis Farr and gave us half a dozen more, all using the names in song titles: "When Derain goes pitter-patter," "Picasso love you," "Joshua blew his trumpet at the walls of Chirico." "Rouault, Rouault, Rouault your boat," and "Matisse this thing called love." You don't like 'em? Well, as Fadiman said, "Degastibus non est disputandum."

---

*Norman Hickman introduced me to this delicious and grievously neglected book, thereby adding another item to the long inventory of my debt to him.

Automobiles, Mostly Early

JOKE, CIRCA 1910:

Knicker: "My car doesn't need a Klaxon. You can always hear it coming. It has a brass band on its radiator."

Bocker: "Mine doesn't need one either. Right up front, it warns you, 'Dodge.'"

Things were so simple and convenient in those days! Our house number was 301 West Franklin Street; our telephone number was Franklin 301; and our automobile plates were 301.

It's hard to feel affection for a modern automobile, such as E. B. White felt for his Model T Ford and described with such nostalgic charm in his "Farewell, My Lovely." Perhaps it's because most of them look like metal muffins, indistinguishable lumps. As a boy, I could identify most cars when they were blocks away: the Pierce-Arrow, with its headlights sunk into its

21

fenders ("mudguards," we called them); the Packard, with its hood like shoulders; the Bugatti, with its oval radiator; the Crane-Simplex, with its roaring, rattling chain drive; the lordly Locomobile, Peerless, and Lozier; the Franklin, with its snowplow radiator (which a local chauffeur described as "lookin' lak a heifer wit' he haid cut off "); the "tin Lizzie," of imperishable fame; and to go far, far back, the Rambler, with its two rear seats facing each other. We entered from the back via a door over the rear axle.

Where are they now? They and their unmistakable silhouettes? Gone! They have melted into the mass of the grandsons of the men who designed the Stutz Bearcat. Now they design cars with the clean lines of a sand castle and the personality of a golf cart. Their goal, their dream, is a roof so low that an average man must crawl in on his hands and knees. Prince Philip, Duke of Edinburgh, recently asked a group of Canadian automobile manufacturers, "Why don't you build one that a fellow can get into without bumping his head?"

Well, why don't you?

My uncle Jonathan's first car, circa 1910, was an E.M.F. The initials represented the manufacturers, Everett, Metzger, and Flanders of Detroit. But a long series of breakdowns led to their being translated as "Every Mechanical Fault."

A scent is now on sale which will give your humble jalopy the rich smell of an English luxury car: a blend of fine leather, burl walnut paneling, and pure wool carpets.

Many automobile manufacturers have named their product for themselves, but R. E. Olds is the only one to name two cars for himself: the Reo and the Oldsmobile. On the other hand, one car, the Rolls-Royce, was named for two men: Charles S. Rolls and Sir Henry Frederick Royce. A plaque in the Midland Hotel, Manchester, England, marks the spot where they first met, in 1910, and went on to form their celebrated partnership.

Nostalgia: Goggles . . . lap robe . . . visored cap (which "sports" turned backward) . . . linen duster and chiffon veil . . .

gauntlets ... leather leggings ... "Cannonball" Baker, Louis Chevrolet, Ralph de Palma ...

Nicknames for the early cars: Pierce-Arrow—"Fierce Sparrow"; Studebaker—"Steady-breaker"; Hupmobile, "Git-up-mobile"; Duesenberg, "Doozie"; Hispano Suiza, "Hizzer-Swizzer"; and, preeminently, "Tin Lizzie."

Legend has it that "Lizzie" is a tribute to Henry Ford's wife, Elizabeth. This is plausible but false. Mrs. Ford's name was Clara Bryant. Lizzie is actually a slang form of "limousine."

The great New York to Paris automobile race, run westward, started on February 12, 1908, and ended 170 days and 12,116 miles later. The winner was the Thomas Flyer, six cylinders, with a top speed of 74 mph.

Joke, circa 1914: Did you ever notice that four of the finest American cars all begin with the letter "P"? Pierce-Arrow, Packard, Peerless, and Puick.

Nostalgia

Isinglass curtains stored under the front seat, where they cracked and split ... a bud vase in limousines ... the straps over the hood ... the thermometer mounted in the radiator cap ... the Prestolite tank on the running board ... the hairpin in the tool kit, for cleaning the gas jets in the headlights ... the hand-pumped Klaxon ... the snare-drum headlights ... the folding windshield ... the brass quadrant mounted on the steering wheel, with spark and speed levers ... the tires with metal studs to turn aside nails and sharp-edged stones ... the shovel for digging out of mudholes ... routes identified by colored stripes on telephone poles ... "Excuse My Dust!"

The French claim to a place in the front rank of pioneer automobile manufacturers is buttressed by the number of French words that survive in our automobile nomenclature. Here are a few of them: chassis, tonneau, garage, coupe, sedan, limousine, carburetor, chauffeur (literally, "someone who heats the engine").

I can't think of many novels in which an automobile plays a major role. First in seniority (if in nothing else) is probably *Tom Swift and His Electric Runabout*, which dates from 1910. Some of Dornford Yates's "clubland" romances, a few years later, feature a sort of all-purpose Rolls-Royce, with enough special equipment for a battalion of Seabees. Another special car was the "twelve-cylinder, eight-liter *Paragon Panther*" owned by "Commander Caractacus Pott, R. N. (Ret.)," as described in Ian Fleming's *Chitty Chitty Bang Bang*.

But surely the most vivid and memorable automobile in fiction is that "long, low, yellow car which shone like a battle chariot. . . . Open as a yacht, it wore a great shining bonnet, and flying over the crest of this great bonnet was that silver stork by which the gentle may know that they have just escaped death beneath the wheels of a Hispano-Suiza."

The car belonged to the wildly wanton Iris March. We make its acquaintance, and hers, in the first few pages of Michael Arlen's 1924 best-seller, *The Green Hat*, and we lose both Iris and her car in the last few pages: "The stork screamed hoarsely, once, twice, thrice. . . . There was a tearing crash, a tongue of fire . . . a grinding, moaning noise as of a great beast in pain. . . . My foot touched something beside the road, and I picked up the green hat."

Here another dream-boat roars out of another Ian Fleming book, *Casino Royale*, and into this one. James Bond, the star intelligence agent, owned the car and cherished it: "One of the last of the $4\frac{1}{2}$-litre Bentleys with the supercharger by Amherst Villiers. . . . It was a battleship-grey convertible . . . and it was capable of touring at ninety with thirty miles an hour in reserve. . . . Bond eased it out of the garage . . . and soon the loitering drumbeat of its exhaust was echoing down the boulevard. . . ."

We're off:—in furious pursuit of assorted villains, all of deepest dye.

Wonderful stuff, eh?

Nostalgia

"Like to go for a spin in my flivver next Sunday afternoon?"

Joke, circa 1919: "What kind of car are you going to buy?" "The only kind I can—a Ford."

Babies

FRIEND: "WINSTON! How wonderfully your new grandson resembles you!"

W.S.C. "All babies look like me. But then, I look like all babies."

KAY HALLE, *Irrepressible Churchill*

Friend: "Do you like babies?"
Noel Coward: "Yes, lightly boiled."

Any man who hates dogs and babies can't be all bad.

W. C. FIELDS

I like [babies] better than I did, if they are nice and pretty.... Abstractedly, I have no tendre [sic] for them till they have become a little human; an ugly baby is a very nasty object—and the prettiest is frightful when undressed—till about four months;

in short, as long as they have their big body and little brains
and that terrible frog-like action.

QUEEN VICTORIA, to her eldest daughter,
Vicky—4 May 1859. *Dearest Child*, edited by ROGER FULFORD

Robert Quillen (1887–1948), the free-wheeling, fire-breathing,
devil-may-care editor of the weekly *Fountain Inn* (S.C.) *Tribune*,
was notorious for printing whatever came into his hot head.
Here is a birth announcement he wrote and ran some sixty years
ago:

> Born on Monday, January 27, to Mr. and Mrs. Jim Dad-
> eright, a son. The little fellow has the community's sincere
> sympathy. On his mother's side are three idiots and one
> jailbird of record, and nobody on the father's side can
> count above four. With that start in life, he faces a world
> that will scorn and abuse and eventually hang him through
> no fault of his own.

There were no such people as the Daderights—rather, there
may have been many such, but none by that name. Quillen was
simply working off a fit of rage and contempt for an area which
he called "illiterate, barbarous and murderous." For more of
Quillen's work, see page 289.

Babies: A loud noise at one end and no sense of responsibility
at the other.

RONALD KNOX

A soiled baby, with a neglected nose, cannot conscientiously be regarded as a thing of beauty.

MARK TWAIN

Baby boys wear blue because it is the color of Heaven and therefore was thought a protection from the Devil. Pink for baby girls may come from an Egyptian fairy tale claiming that girls were born out of pink roses.

A Pennsylvania folktale says that before a baby is born, it knows all the secrets of life and death; but at the moment of its birth, an angel presses his forefinger against its upper lip, sealing it, and leaving the small vertical crease (philtrum) that we all carry for the rest of our lives.

The average baby weighs about 7½ pounds at birth, yet in 1961 there was born in Turkey a baby boy who weighed 24 pounds 4 ounces.

UNIVERSAL PRESS SYNDICATE

Barroom Bets
(CONT'D)

How MANY EYES are there on the jacks in a deck of cards? Well, two of the jacks, spades and hearts, have one eye each, and the other two have two eyes each, making six. But wait: each jack has two faces, so the correct answer is twelve.

How many grooves are there on one side of an LP record? Answer: One. It is continuous.

Can you recite the Lord's Prayer *correctly*? Here it is from Matthew 6: 9–13:
Our Father, which art in heaven, Hallowed be thy name. Thy kingdom come. Thy will be done in earth, as it is in heaven. Give us this day our daily bread: And forgive us our debts, as we forgive our debtors. And lead us not into temptation, but deliver us from evil: For thine is the kingdom, and the power, and the glory, for ever. Amen.

People who try to recite it usually leave out the "and" after "debtors." It might be wise to have the prayer copied and notarized.

Was there ever born in the United States a monarch who inherited the throne and reigned? Yes. King Bhumibol Adulyadej Rama IX of Thailand was born in Cambridge, Massachusetts, on December 5, 1927.

Would you bet that you do *not* know at least twenty-five words of Russian? You'd probably lose. Consider this list:

Czar, czarina, czarevitch
Bolshevik, menshevik,
Duma, soviet, commissar,
vodka, blini, samovar, borsch,
troika, verst, dacha, steppe, kulak,
boyar, babushka,
glasnost, sputnik, ruble, kopeck.
Da (yes), *nyet* (NO!!!!!)

That's twenty-five. For good measure, here are a few more perhaps less familiar: *samizdat* (underground publication), *chai* (tea), *spasibo* (thank you), *tovarich* (comrade), and *do svidaniya* (goodbye).

(Note: *Caviar* is *not* a Russian word; the Russian for *caviar* is *ikra*.)

How quickly can you find out what is unusual about this paragraph? It looks so ordinary that you'd think nothing was wrong with it at all, and, in fact, nothing is. But it is unusual. Why? If you study it and think about it, you may find out, but you must do it without coaching. No doubt if you work at it for long, it will dawn on you. Go to work and try your skill. Par is about half an hour.

(There is no *e* in the paragraph.)
News Bulletin of Central Intelligence Retirees Association

Would you bet that peacocks do *not* lay eggs? They don't, but peahens do.

The Bible
(CONT'D)

"For whosoever hath, to him shall be given . . . but whosoever hath not, from him shall be taken away even that he hath." (Matthew 13:12). Isn't this an Irish bull?

Look up II Chronicles 36:9: "Jehoiachin was eight years old when he began to reign, and he reigned three months and ten days in Jerusalem; and he did that which was evil in the sight of the Lord." What *could* the poor imp have done? I suppose he catapulted [i.e., hit with a slingshot] the postman's dog or something of the sort. . . .

The Lyttleton Hart-Davis Letters

"The Breeches Bible" is the one in which Genesis 3:7 is translated "They sewed figge-tree leaves together, and made themselves breeches" (not "aprons").

"The Bug Bible" tells the reader not to "be afraid for any bugges by night."

"The Vinegar Bible" has a chapter heading (Matthew 20) which reads "The parable of the Vinegar" instead of "the Vineyard."

"The Treacle Bible" asks "Is there no treacle in Gilead?" instead of "balm." (Jeremiah 8:22)

The word "whale" appears nowhere in the Bible. Jonah was swallowed up by "a great fish." (Jonah 1:17)

Nor does the word "snake" appear; "serpent," yes, several dozen times, but not "snake."

"God tempers the wind to the shorn lamb" is not in the Bible, but in Laurence Sterne's *A Sentimental Journey*.

The Bible does not say "Money is the root of all evil," but the "Love of money," etc. (Timothy 6:10)

Nor does the Bible tell the story of Susannah and the Elders; it is in the Apocrypha.

> There are few exemplars of bonhomie
> In the book of Deuteronomy.
>
> Anon.

The Bible says, "The race is not to the swift, nor the battle to the strong" (Ecclesiastes 9:11), but that's the way the wise money bets.

DAMON RUNYON

Scriptures: The sacred books of a holy religion, as distinguished from the false and profane writings on which all other faiths are based.

AMBROSE BIERCE

The Bible tells us to love our neighbors and also to love our enemies; probably because they are generally the same people.

MARK TWAIN

"Shakspeare" is one of the various ways in which he spelled his name—in two syllables, of four and six letters respectively. Open your King James version of the Bible to the forty-sixth Psalm. The forty-sixth word from the beginning is "shake"— and the forty-sixth word from the end is "spear."

JOHN R. COURNYER

Reader, do you wonder, as I do, how on earth anyone ever made this astonishing discovery?

When Emperor Menelik II of Ethiopia wasn't feeling well, he tore a page from the Bible and ate it.

The Bible is literature, not dogma.

GEORGE SANTAYANA

Fear is the denomination of the Old Testament; belief is the denomination of the New.

BENJAMIN WHICHCOTE

Book Titles

WHAT FOLLOWS is a list not of favorite books, but of favorite book *titles*. Some are on my own shelves; others were sent in by friends whom I had solicited for nominations; all, I think, are inviting, arresting, seductive, and/or provocative. What man could resist picking up a book called *An Armful of Warm Girl?* Not I!

Jaws, Peter Benchley
Goodbye to All That, Robert Graves
Paradise Lost, John Milton
An Armful of Warm Girl, W. M. Spackman
Beautiful Women, Ugly Scenes, C. D. B. Bryan
Treasure Island, Robert Louis Stevenson
The Joy of Sex, edited by Alexander Comfort
Murder on the Orient Express, Agatha Christie
"The Girls in Their Summer Dresses," (a short story), Irwin Shaw

Lady into Fox, David Garnett
Vanity Fair, W. M. Thackeray
The Sea, the Sea, Iris Murdoch
A Lost Lady, Willa Cather
A Handful of Dust, Evelyn Waugh
The Man Who Was Thursday, G. K. Chesterton
The Burning Fountain, Eleanor Carroll Chilton
The Gentle Art of Making Enemies, James McNeill Whistler
Besides, the Wench Is Dead, Davenport

Cast of Characters

IN JAMES JOYCE's *Ulysses*, he mentions "Lord Winterbottom, a cold, stern man." The little joke inspired a group of us to compose other such names. For instance:

The fattest girl in town, Ella van Tass; a chaplain, the Rev. Evans A. Bove; a gardener, Pete Morse; the office clock watcher, Willis Scarlett O'Day; a shyster, Abe S. Carpis, and his secretary, Effie David. These last led to some high-powered, big-league law firms: Taggart, Taggart, Byrne & Bright and Howard, Jalecki, Polk & de Puss (credit John Falter). Here we realized that we had strayed from the original game—names as identifications—and were merely stringing words together, so we tried to organize a Little Theater stock company:

The Juvenile . . . . Gellish Lofter
The Soubrette . . . . Ginny Breth
The Heavy . . . . Curtius Foyle Duganne

The Leading Lady . . . . Natalie Kladd
The Character Man . . . . Seth M. Ortlebard

That last one showed strain,and since we couldn't come up with an ingénue at all, (a possibility has just come to me: How about Mabel Sirrop?), we quit, after agreeing that our two masterpieces were:

AUBER & WEIR

LANDSCAPE ARCHITECTS

TARNS AND WOODLANDS A SPECIALTY

and Hugh Troy's brilliant:

SHIRLEY, GOODNESS & MURPHY

PRIVATE DETECTIVES

"WE FOLLOW YOU ALL THE DAYS OF YOUR LIFE"

It didn't occur to us until long afterward that our game was a development of the early English playwrights' convention whereby they gave their characters names that were tags or labels. The bawd in Shakespeare's *King Henry IV*, Doll Tearsheet, is one of the best known, and there are scores of others. Garrick has "Fribble, a coxcomb" in his *Miss in Her Tears* (1747), and Sheridan has Lord Foppington in his *A Trip to Scarborough* (1777). Dickens put several such into *Nicholas Nickleby*: Lord

37

Frederick Verisopht, Mr. Snobb, and the good-humored Cheery-
ble brothers. He was a master at christening his characters.
"Uriah Heep" and "Edward Murdstone" tell us all we need to
know about them before they've spoken a word.

A final note: George Kaufman played the game with menus.
Two of his "dishes" were a cowardly mafioso, "Chicken" Cac-
ciatore, and a race-track tout, "Potatoes" O'Brien. Elaine Stein-
beck gave us a chorus girl, "Cherries" Jubilee, and Rosemary
Dyer contributed a French movie star, Blanquette de Veau. Me,
I'm proud of my heavyweight wrestler, "Beef" Wellington.

P.S.: Should we add Congressman Philip Buster?

Christmas

"I AM AS LIGHT as a feather. I am as happy as an angel. I am as merry as a schoolboy. I am as giddy as a drunken man. A merry Christmas to everybody! Hallo, there! Whoop! Hallo!"

So began a memorable day for the reformed miser, Ebenezer Scrooge, in Dickens's *A Christmas Carol*.

"At last the anchor was up, the sails were set, and off we glided. It was a short, cold Christmas; and as the short northern day merged into night, we found ourselves almost broad upon the wintry ocean, whose freezing spray cased us in ice, as in polished armor."

So began a memorable voyage for Ishmael and the *Pequod*, in Melville's *Moby Dick*.

Also born on Christmas Day:
Sir Isaac Newton, Mrs. William Wordsworth, Clara Barton (founder of the American Red Cross), Steve Brodie (who

jumped from the Brooklyn Bridge and survived), Robert "Believe It or Not" Ripley, Humphrey Bogart, Rebecca West, Cab Calloway, Tony Martin, Paul Manship (sculptor), Clark Clifford, Evangeline Booth, Conrad Hilton.

Saint Nicholas, a fourth-century bishop of Myra, in Asia Minor, is the patron saint of children, virgins, sailors, thieves, and pawnbrokers, and also of Greece, Russia, and Sicily. Nicholas shouldn't be confused with the patron saint of golfers, Nicklaus.

On Christmas Day 1818, in Oberndorf, Austria, "Silent Night, Holy Night" was sung for the first time; it had been composed only the evening before.

Christmas is a holiday that persecutes the lonely, the frayed, and the rejected.

JIMMY CANNON

Santa Claus has the right idea; visit people once a year.

VICTOR BORGE

Both Charlemagne, King of the Franks, and William the Conqueror were crowned on Christmas Day. Charlemagne in 800, William in 1066.

Christmas is only for servants.

EMERALD CUNARD

In Sweden, people tie sheaves of grain to long poles and mount them near their homes for the birds. They believe that if the birds eat the grain, the next harvest will be good.

On Christmas Day 1776, Washington crossed the Delaware.

I salute you! There is nothing I can give you which you have not, but there is much that while I cannot give, you can take.
No heaven can come to us unless our hearts find rest in it today. Take Heaven.
No peace lies in the future which is not hidden in this present instant. Take Peace.

The gloom of the world is but a shadow; behind it, yet within our reach, is joy. Take Joy.

And so, at this Christmas time, I greet you with the prayer that for you, now and forever, the day breaks and the shadows flee away.

FRA ANGELICO, 1513

Thanksgiving comes *after* Christmas for people over thirty.

PETER KREEFT, *A Turn of the Clock*

The opera *La Bohème* begins on Christmas Eve.

Ian Robertson Hamilton, now an eminent Queen's Counsel, celebrated Christmas Eve 1956 by stealing the Stone of Scone (also known as the Stone of Destiny and the Ciribatuib Stone) from Westminster Abbey.

A friend: "Did you hang up your stocking on Christmas Eve?"

Dorothy Parker: "No, I hung up my hotel."

Whereas we hang up our stockings, children in Italy, Spain, and France put out their shoes to be filled with gifts on January 6.

I am sorry to have to introduce the subject of Christmas. It is an indecent subject; a cruel, gluttonous subject; a drunken, disorderly subject; a wasteful, disastrous subject; a wicked, cadging, lying, filthy, blasphemous and demoralizing subject. Christmas is forced on a reluctant and disgusted nation by the shopkeepers and the press. On its own merits it would wither and shrivel in the fiery breath of universal hatred; and anyone who looked back to it would be turned into a pillar of greasy sausages.

GEORGE BERNARD SHAW

I believed in Christmas until I was eight years old. I had saved up some money carrying ice in Philadelphia, and I was going to buy my mother a copper-bottomed clothes boiler for Christmas. I kept the money hidden in a brown crock in the coal bin. My father found the crock. He did exactly what I would have done in his place. He stole the money. And ever since then I've remembered nobody on Christmas, and I want nobody to remember me either.

w. c. fields

Fields always referred to Death as "that fellow in the bright nightgown," and he always hated and dreaded Christmas. It is ironic that when "that fellow" came for him in 1946, it was on Christmas Day.

[Saint] Nicholas, born in Patara [Turkey] around A.D. 300, achieved fame by resurrecting three children whom a butcher had cut up and put in brine. His association with children was matched by that for gift-giving: hearing of a man, once wealthy, but now fallen on hard times, who was unable to find dowries for his three daughters, Nicholas entered the house secretly by night and left three purses of gold. Hence the three daughters were able to contract suitable marriages and avoid a more public fate. Many stories are told of Nicholas' miraculous powers in rescuing prisoners, shipwrecked sailors, lost travellers, recovering lost property, and generally answering the prayers of those in distress. Now, 1700 years later, his cult has reached alarming proportions among children, who await his beneficence each Christmas morning.

diana darke, *Guide to Aegean and Mediterranean Turkey*

St. Nicholas was buried in the crypt of his church at Myra, in Turkey, but in 1087 his bones were stolen by some Italian sailors, who reburied them at Bari, on the east coast of Italy. They are still there.

We shall soon have Christmas at our throats.

p. g. wodehouse, "Jeeves and the Downy Bird"

On Christmas Day 1497, Vasco da Gama, cruising the southeast coast of Africa, sighted a bay and named the country behind it "Natal" to commemorate the date. On Christmas 1774, Captain James Cook came upon a sound which he named "Christmas." And on Christmas Day, 1777, he did the same for an island in the Indian Ocean.

Annie H. Ide (later Mrs. W. Bourke Cochran) was born on December 25, 1881. In 1892, when her father was U.S. land commissioner in Samoa, young Annie protested to Robert Louis Stevenson, then resident there, against the unfairness of having one's birthday fall on Christmas Day. Stevenson promptly drew up a solemn document that gave all his "rights and privileges in the thirteenth day of November, formerly my birthday, and hereby and henceforth [hers], to have, hold, exercise, enjoy ... by the sporting of fine raiment, eating of rich meats, and receipt of gifts, compliments, and copies of verse. ..."

Colors
(CONT'D)

BROWN IS THE ONLY major color that doesn't appear in the spectrum.

> Blue is true,
> Yellow is jealous,
> Green's forsaken,
> Red's brazen,
> White is love,
> And black is earth.
> > Folklore from the east of England.

A tailor is speaking: "Scarlet, such as is used for regimentals, is the most blinding of all colors. It seems to burn the eyeballs and makes them ache dreadful.... Everything seems all of a twitter, and to keep changing the tint. There's more military tailors blind than any others."

ROBERT HUGHES,
The Fatal Shore: The Epic of Australia's Founding

The human eye can distinguish among some 10 million hues and shades.

[Lord Petersham, 1780–1851] His carriages were unique of their kind; they were entirely brown, with brown horses and harness. The groom was dressed in a long brown coat. . . . It is said that Lord Petersham's devotion to brown was caused by his having been desperately in love with a very beautiful widow bearing that name.

The Reminiscences and Recollections of Captain Gronow

People who love yellow are usually happy and harmless.

PETER KREEFT, *A Turn of the Clock*

Why is a rage *red?* A funk *blue?* A study *brown?* A healthy condition *pink?* Sins *scarlet?* The eyes of jealousy *green?*

I've been forty years discovering that the queen of all colors is black.

AUGUSTE RENOIR

Mauve is just pink trying to be purple.

JAMES MCNEILL WHISTLER

Verde que te quiero verde,
Verde viento, verde ramas.*

FEDERICO GARCÍA LORCA

In Korea, mourners wear white. Also in China.

Libya is the only country to have a flag that is a solid color: green.

---

*Green how I love you green
Green wind, green branches.

Conversation
(CONT'D)

TALK TO EVERY WOMAN as if you loved her, and to every man as if he bored you, and at the end of your first season you will have the reputation of possessing the most perfect social tact.

OSCAR WILDE, *The Picture of Dorian Gray*

Good morning, Algernon. Good morning, Percy.
Good morning, Mrs. Roebuck. Christ have mercy!

HILAIRE BELLOC, *Sonnets and Verses*

Great talkers are so constituted that they do not know their own thoughts until, on the tide of their particular gift, they hear them issuing from their mouths.

THORNTON WILDER

Sir, you have but two topics, yourself and me. I am sick of both.

DR. SAMUEL JOHNSON

I never desire to converse with a man who has written more than he has read.

IB.

He is not only dull himself, he is the cause of dullness in others.

IB.

Your ignorance cramps my conversation.

ANTHONY HOPE HAWKINS

Silence is the unbearable repartee.

G. K. CHESTERTON

When you stick on conversation's burrs,
Don't strew your pathway with those dreadful ers.

OLIVER WENDELL HOLMES

ers, urs, and you know, like I said, y'unnerstan, very-very or what have you ... at any rate ... in other words ... this, that and the other ... and all such conversational excelsior.

The trouble with her is that she lacks the power of conversation but not the power of speech.

GEORGE BERNARD SHAW

If other people are going to talk, conversation becomes impossible.

JAMES MCNEILL WHISTLER

During the Samuel Johnson days, they had big men enjoying small talk. Now we have small men enjoying big talk.

FRED ALLEN

Look wise, say nothing and grunt. Speech was given to conceal thought.

SIR WILLIAM OSLER

He has occasional flashes of silence that makes his conversation perfectly delightful!

SYDNEY SMITH, of Macaulay

He not only overflowed with learning, but stood in the slop.

IB.

It is time to stop talking when the other person nods, but says nothing.

Anon.

If you have nothing pleasant to say about anyone, come and sit by me.

ALICE ROOSEVELT LONGWORTH

An affectation of wit by degrees hardens the heart, and spoils good company and good manners. A perpetual succession of good things puts an end to common conversation. There is no answer to a jest, but another; and even where the ball can be kept up in this way without ceasing, it tires the patience of the by-standers, and runs the speakers out of breath. Wit is the salt of conversation, not the food.

WILLIAM HAZLITT

The first law of repartee: Better never than late.

Anon.

What do women like to talk most? Gossip.
What do men like to talk most? Shop.

Costumes
and Fashions
(CONT'D)

FINIS FARR SAID that his friend Gilmer Black had a suit of a pattern so bold that he had to wear two pair of trousers to get it all in.

The bowler had a low, rounded crown. William Coke of Norfolk is said to have invented it and at Locke's hat shop in St. James's Street, it is still referred to as a "William Coke hat." In popular parlance this became a "billycocke." The first examples were actually made by a craftsman named Bowler, and this was the name that finally stuck to it.

JAMES LAVER, *Dandies*

Apparel named for persons: bloomers, wellingtons, bluchers, spencer, chesterfield, Prince Albert, mackintosh, bowler . . . and for places: Tuxedo, homburg, Panama, Inverness, ascot, Ulster, derby, cravat (Croatia).

50

The captain of *H.M.S. Blazer* in the 1860s outfitted his crew in striped T-shirts and bandannas, with dark blue jackets with three patch pockets and metal buttons. Hence the "blazer."

Beau Brummell's tailors were Davidson & Meyer.

In the days before Baudelaire abandoned dandyism, he used to wear rose-pink gloves.

When Elisabeth von Wittelsbach of Bavaria became Empress of Austria-Hungary, she found that she was expected never to wear a pair of shoes more than once, and six times at the absolute maximum.

A well-dressed lady has a sense of inward tranquillity which religion is powerless to bestow.

> Attributed to a MISS C. F. FORBES,
> by Emerson in *Social Aims*

It is strange that men can esteem no other creatures but themselves for qualities alien to them. We praise a horse for its strength and not its harness; a greyhound for its speed and not its color. Why don't we, in like manner, value a man for what is properly his? The pedestal is no part of the statue. Let a man lay aside his revenues and stand in his shirt. When we consider a king a peasant, a nobleman and a villain, a rich man and a poor man, we are immediately taken by the disparity between them, the only difference is the cut of the breeches.

> MONTAIGNE

I read this somewhere years ago, and have treasured it ever since:

A distraught woman burst into a millinery shop and seized the proprietor's arm. "Help me!" she begged. She managed to explain that she was on her way to a wedding. A few steps from the church, her hat had blown off and a taxi had run over it, utterly ruining it. Please, could the milliner give her something chic, and *at once?* He glanced at her costume, chose a spool of silk ribbon, unrolled a couple of yards, twirled it into a sort of double bow, pinned it, and handed it to her. "There you are, madam. Will that do?"

The woman cried, "Why, it's beautiful, simply *beautiful*! Thank you. How much do I owe you?"

"Fifty dollars, madam."

"*Fifty dollars?* For a simple piece of ribbon? Outrageous!"

He took it from her, removed the pins, and shook it out. "No, madam," he said, handing it back, "the ribbon is free."

Elegance is good taste, plus a dash of daring.
                    CARMEL SNOW, former editor of *Harper's Bazaar*

Before 1800, shoes for the right and left foot were interchangeable.

Pete Martin, an associate editor of the old *Saturday Evening Post*, was interviewing Mrs. Fred Lasswell, in preparation for an article about her husband, the creator of the "Moon Mullins" comic strip. It soon became clear that Lasswell was much like Mullins, a raucous, rough-and-tumble sort of fellow, happiest in taverns and pool parlors.

Pete asked Mrs. Lasswell, "Does Fred ever dress for dinner?"
She thought for a moment. "Well, sometimes he puts on a clean sweatshirt."

Nostalgia (men)

Scarfpins ... spats and gaiters ... white piping on waistcoats ... Prince Alberts ... watch chains, watch fobs, watch charms ... high-button shoes ... Norfolk jackets ... Oxford bags ... detachable cuffs ... Eton collars ... walking sticks ... plus fours ... long stockings and sailor suits (for boys) ... derbies ... Windsor ties ... sleeve garters ... knickerbockers ... silk hats ... a feather in the hatband ... celluloid collars ... buttons of knotted leather ... boaters ... monocles ...

[*The Wizard of Oz*] made sixteen-year-old Judy Garland an international star. Thirty years after, the ruby slippers she wore as Dorothy brought $15,000 at an auction. Bert Lahr's Cowardly Lion costume brought $3,400, almost twice as much as the winning bid for Clark Gable's trench coat. And in June 1988, another of the six original pairs of ruby slippers sold for $165,000.

WILLIAM CHILDRESS, "On the Road to Oz," *Ford Times*

You'd be surprised how expensive it is to look as cheap as this.

DOLLY PARTON

How do fashions (or fads) start? Well, when King Edward VII's increasing paunch suggested that he ease the strain on his waistcoat by leaving its bottom button undone, fashionable London men were quick to follow the royal lead.

[I was] told of Coleridge riding about in a strange, shabby dress with I forget whom, and on some company approaching them, Coleridge offered to fall behind and pass for his companion's servant. "No," said the other. "I am proud of you as a friend; but I must say, I should be ashamed of you as a servant."

TOM MOORE, *Journal*

Nostalgia (women)

Spit curls ... "teddy bears" ... beauty patches ... leg of mutton sleeves ... hats with ostrich feathers ... lace collars and cuffs ... "cootie garages" ... guimpes ... Mother Hubbards ... galoshes ... jabots ... corset covers ... lavallières ... shirtwaists ... bloomers ... chatelaine watches ... camisoles ... "rainy-daisy" skirts ... bustles ... hobble skirts ... lorgnettes ... fans ... berthas ... dress shields ... middy blouses ... step-ins ... hug-me-tights ... tiaras ... "dog collars" ... knickers ... chemises ... drawers ... hatpins ... veils ... boas ... opera-length gloves.

The Cruel Critics
(CONT'D)

SOME CRITICISMS of Jenny Lind:

Thackeray: "I was thinking of something else the whole time she was jugulating away."

Hawthorne: "I was not very much interested in her."

Walt Whitman: "There was a vacuum in the head of the performance. It was the beauty of Adam before God breathed into his nostrils."

Carlyle: "I do not deign to hear Lind again; it would not bring me sixpence worth of benefit, I think, to hear her sing six months in that kind of material."

Dorothy Parker, on *The House Beautiful*, a play by Channing Pollock: "*The House Beautiful* is the play lousy."

From a review of a pianist's performance: "He has Van Gogh's ear for music."

Tallulah Bankhead, of a Maeterlinck play: "There's less to this than meets the eye."

Mr. Henry James writes fiction as if it were a painful duty.
OSCAR WILDE

This is not a novel to be tossed aside lightly; it should be thrown with great force.
DOROTHY PARKER

[Professor] Porson, hearing someone observe that "certain modern poets would be read and admired when Homer and Virgil were forgotten," made answer . . . "and not till then!"
WILLIAM HAZLITT, *The English Comic Writers*

The scenery in the play was beautiful, but the actors got in front of it.
ALEXANDER WOOLLCOTT

I am sitting in the smallest room in my house [i.e. the W.C.]. . . . I have your review in front of me. Soon it will be behind me.
MAX REGER, a German composer, to a music critic

The play was so bad, even the ushers hissed.
BURLE WILKINSON

Virginia Woolf, of E. M. Forster's *A Room With a View*: "The view is smaller than we expected."

Meredith is a prose Browning, and so is Browning.
OSCAR WILDE

The audience hissed Charles Lamb's play so savagely that he joined in, for fear that he might be identified as the author.

Dorothy Parker, in Tallulah Bankhead's dressing-room after an opening: "Tallulah, your show is slipping."

Your manuscript is both good and original, but the part that is good is not original, and the part that is original is not good.

DR. SAMUEL JOHNSON

If you were to ask me what [Anton Chekhov's play] *Uncle Vanya* is about, I would have to say about as much as I can take.

ROBERT GARLAND, *New York Journal-American*

In one place in *Deerslayer*, and in the restricted space of two-thirds of a page, [James Fenimore] Cooper has scored 114 offences against literary art out of a possible 115. It breaks the record.

MARK TWAIN, *How to Tell a Story and Other Essays*

Le Figaro, of Gustave Flaubert's *Madame Bovary*: "Monsieur Flaubert is not a writer."

[Herman Melville's *Moby Dick*] is a large dose of hyperbolical slang, maudlin sentimentalism and tragic-comic bubble and squeak.

W. HARRISON AINSWORTH, *New Monthly Magazine*

[*Hamlet*] is a vulgar and barbarous drama, which would not be tolerated by the vilest populace of France, or Italy.... One would imagine this piece to be the work of a drunken savage.

VOLTAIRE

Of a musical with plagiarized tunes: "This show was the kind of play where you whistle the tunes going into the theatre."

George S. Kaufman began one of his reviews, "There was laughter in the back of the theater, leading to the belief that someone was telling jokes back there."

The Comte de Rivarol's criticism of a two-line poem: "Very nice, but there are dull stretches."

Evelyn Waugh's style has the desperate jauntiness of an orchestra fiddling away for dear life on a sinking ship.

EDMUND WILSON

Wilson's scorn may have been influenced by Waugh's refusal to give him an interview. Waugh was notorious for his hatred of Americans and his contempt for them. When I was living in Rome in 1954, I used to go to the American church on the Via Napoli most Sundays, and after the service, to the bar of the Grand Hotel nearby, for two magnificent martinis. One Sunday, as I was leaving, I saw Waugh's unmistakable porcine face and crimson complexion at a table by the door. I weighed my wish to express my admiration for his writings against the probability of his rudeness, and this is what happened:
Self: "Mr. Waugh, allow me to thank you for the pleasure your books have given me."
Waugh: "How veddy kaind! Have we met?"
Self: "No." Exit.

Asking a working writer what he thinks of critics is like asking a lamppost what it thinks of dogs.

Anon.

George Bernard Shaw, of *Gounod's Redemption*: If you will only take the precaution to go in long enough after it commences and to come out long enough before it is over, you will not find it wearisome.

58

Deaths, Strange and Violent
(CONT'D)

HYPATIA OF ALEXANDRIA, a mathematician and neo-Platonist, was cut to death with oyster shells by Christian monks in 415.

It takes a hanged man 20 minutes to die.
STUART A. SANDOW, Durations

Euripides was killed by a pack of hunting dogs, 406 B.C.

[Jehu] said, Throw her down. So they threw [Jezebel] down [from the window] and some of her blood was sprinkled on the wall, and on the horses: and he trode her under foot ... and he ... said, go, see this cursed woman and bury her ... but they found no more of her than the skull, and the feet, and the palms of her hands.
II Kings 9:33–35

[The headsman's] first blow missed the neck of [Mary, Queen of Scots] and cut into the back of the head. The queen's lips

59

moved, and servants thought they heard the whispered words, "Sweet Jesus." The second blow severed the neck, all but the smallest sinew and this was severed by using the axe as a saw.... The executioner now held aloft the dead woman's head.... The lips still moved and continued to do so for a quarter of an hour.

ANTONIA FRASER, *Mary Queen of Scots*

When the Moors captured Gibraltar in 711, they crucified each soldier of the garrison upside down, between a crucified dog and a crucified pig.

Death did not occur in the incident that follows, but it came very, very close, and under circumstances so extraordinary— even, I daresay, unique—that I feel justified in citing them. I take them from a letter in the May 1988 *Smithsonian*, in which Roger H. Olson writes of the Great Blizzard of 1888:

One man was caught in the storm while he was driving cattle to the river. When it struck, he happened to have a large knife, so he killed a big ox, gutted it, and crawled inside. By morning the flesh and hide was frozen and he could not get out until help came.

The angel of the Lord smote [Herod] . . . and he was eaten of worms, and gave up the ghost.

Acts 12:23

King George I of Greece died from a monkey's bite, in 1913.

[Tommy] climbed the wall, but, as he was descending, one of the iron spikes on the top of it pierced his coat which was buttoned to the throat, and he hung there by the neck. He struggled as he choked, but he could not help himself. He was unable to cry out. The collar of the coat held him fast. . . . He had been dead for some time when they found him.

JAMES M. BARRIE, Tommy and Grizel

Distinctions
(CONT'D)

HORSES SWEAT, men perspire, ladies get all aglow.

A *golf links*, as distinguished from a *golf course*, is one that adjoins water, preferably the sea.

A journalist is a newspaperman who wears spats, but no socks (c. 1910).

A copy is an imitation or transcript of something original. A reproduction is a copy in another medium—e.g., a painted reproduction of a photo. A duplicate is an exact copy, identical, a facsimile. A replica is a copy by the original artist. You could have a replica of a statue, a reproduction of the Declaration of Independence.

Between a *newspaper editor* and a *scientist*: An editor knows less and less about more and more; a scientist knows more and more about less and less.

Slumber and *sleep*: *Slumber* is a light, fitful doze, not the other way around, as I had thought. Psalm 121:7 makes the distinction: "He that keepeth Israel shall neither slumber nor sleep."

Doctors and
Medicine

A DOCTOR FRIEND of mine, a specialist in pulmonary complaints, was consulted by a beauteous young actress, who had become alarmed by her persistent cough. He asked her to remove the top of her dress and her bra, which she did, revealing a glorious bosom. He pressed his ear to it and ordered, "Count one, two, three . . ."

What follows was told me not by my friend, the doctor, but by his thoroughly disrespectful daughter. "Next thing Daddy knew," she said, "the girl was counting 'two hundred and sixty-seven, two hundred and sixty-eight, two hundred and . . .'"

Recent research shows that cold viruses remain active on bathroom tissue for one hour, on the hands for two hours, and on "hard, polished surfaces" for seventy-two hours.

WILLIAM S. SIMS, JR.

Research also shows that colds are spread not so much by sneezing and coughing as by rubbing the eyes with virus-laden fingers. I have therefore taken to pressing elevator buttons with the knuckle of my forefinger.

IB.

A doctor's reputation is made by the number of eminent men who have died under his care.

GEORGE BERNARD SHAW

More tonsillectomies are performed annually in the United States than any other operation. Second are abortions: 900,000 a year.

Biarritz once had a celebrated *guérisseur* (healer) who specialized in the cure of *zona* (shingles). He took the sufferer on his back and marched around his office, chanting, "*Zona, zona, êtes-vous là?*" After the third circuit, he asked the question once more, then cried, "*Alors, va-t'en!*" and dropped the patient, presumably healed.

A. F.

Ketchup was once sold as a medicine.

Nantucket Inquirer and Mirror

The world's largest drugstore is the Pharmacie Principale, in Geneva.

Doctors are men who prescribe medicines of which they know little, to cure disease of which they know less, in human beings of whom they know nothing.

VOLTAIRE

One finger in the throat and one in the rectum makes a good diagnostician.

SIR WILLIAM OSLER

The person most often late for a doctor's appointment is the doctor himself.

Anon.

"Daddy, when Cleopatra was bitten by that asp, why didn't they give her aspirin?"

Dogs

HEGEL, BEETHOVEN, Schubert, Schopenhauer, and [Theodor] Mundt [German novelist] all had poodles. It is alleged that Beethoven and Schubert tried out several musical pieces on their dogs before anyone else heard them. . . . Sigmund Freud's chow, Jo-Fi, was always with him and "screened his patients."

DR. GLENN L. RADDE

The average dog is about as smart as a child three to four years old.

It costs about $400 a year to keep a dog of average size.

Queen Elizabeth II's corgi mated with a dachshund. She called the offspring "dorgies."

Two dogs were hanged for witchcraft in Salem, Massachusetts.

When you point out something to a dog, he looks at your finger.

A spitz, Pomero, used to sit on the head of poet Walter Savage Landor.

When Ellen Glasgow, the Richmond novelist, died, her beloved Sealyham, Jeremy, who had died some years before, was disinterred and placed in her own casket and reburied in Hollywood Cemetery, Richmond.

Labradors have the gentlest, sweetest dispositions of any breed. I have had Junie, Dinah, Mr. Tambo, Missy, "the Labradorable Sassy," and Dixie. Dixie's manners would have been perfect, but for one fault: when she was left alone in the car, she would chew on the armrests. We finally found a simple way to break her, and I commend it to all of you with a similar problem. Ask your friendly neighborhood pharmacist for a one-ounce bottle of a thumb-sucking cure such as THUM. Paint it on the armrests, or on anything else your dog finds appetizing, and we guarantee that his next nibble will cure him.

Immediately after Mary Queen of Scots was beheaded, a strange and pathetic memorial to that devotion which she had always aroused in those who knew her intimately, was discovered: Her little lap dog, a Skye terrier, who had managed to accompany her under her long skirts, had now crept out from beneath her petticoats and in its distress, had stationed itself between the severed head and the shoulders of the body. Nor could it be coaxed away, but steadfastly and uncomprehendingly clung to the solitary thing that it could find which still reminded it of its dead mistress.

ANTONIA FRASER, *Mary Queen of Scots*

When the French captured Lisbon in 1809, one of their first acts was to round up and slaughter some 10,000 stray dogs.

I once shared an office with a murderer. He had served his sentence and was free again, harmless and quite congenial. I have forgotten whom he murdered, and where and how, but I remember clearly a story he told me:

The prison warden sent for him one day and announced that he had been given a puppy, a Dalmatian. "You're an educated man," he said. "How about coming up with a good name for him? I don't want to call him Rex or Rover or Fido or anything cheap like that. I want something *classy*."

My friend asked for the run of the prison library, and "classy" suggesting "classical," he ransacked the *Dictionary of Phrase and Fable, Bulfinch's Mythology*, and a dozen other such sources for the names of glorious dogs of old. He listed Asbolus ("Soot-colored"), Icarius's Maera ("Glistener"), Orion's Arctophonus ("Bear-killer") and Geryon's Orthus and Gargittius, whom Hercules slew in his Tenth Labor. From classic literature he borrowed Kabes, who was tried for stealing cheese in Aristophanes's *The Wasps*, and from ancient history, Peritas, for whom Alexander the Great named a city in India. Welsh legend gave my friend Llewellyn's Gelert, Irish legend, Finn MacCool's Brann and Sgeilen, and in the legend of the Seven Sleepers of Ephesus, he found Katmir (sometimes as the anagram "Kratim"), the dog who stood guard over them for 230 years. Another watchdog came from the Koran: Al Rakim, whom Mohammed admitted to Paradise.

My friend said his final list totaled some three dozen names, each hallowed by the centuries. He sent it to the warden with pride and awaited his choice with impatience. A few days later, he heard the warden's whistle and then his call: "Spot! Spot! Here, Spot!"

A Swiss breeder produced a Newfoundland dog with the legs of a dachshund.

If I have any belief about immortality, it is that certain dogs I have known will go to Heaven, and very, very few persons.

JAMES THURBER

Before you try to pat a strange dog, always let it smell your hand. And Thoreau recommends that when a dog runs at you, you should whistle to him.

Dogs reach sexual maturity at eight months.

There are no bloodhounds in *Uncle Tom's Cabin*. The only reference to them is when Eliza, about to cross the ice, exclaims, "Powers of mercy protect me! How shall I escape these human bloodhounds?"

According to the U.S. Public Health Service, the three breeds least likely to bite are golden retriever, Labrador, and Shetland sheepdog. The ones most likely are chow, poodle, and German shepherd.

In the old *Our Gang* (*Little Rascals*) comedies, the bull terrier with the black circle around his right eye was named Pete.

The various dogs that played "Lassie" in the movies were all males; none was a bitch.

The great pleasure of a dog is that you may make a fool of yourself with him, and not only will he not scold you, but he will make a fool of himself too.

SAMUEL BUTLER

Training a dog for a job with Seeing Eye begins at seven weeks.

I firmly believe that some dogs can read minds. Dixie, my Labrador, usually joins me at breakfast, and I usually give her a scrap of toast or bacon. I have often noticed that when I *decide* to choose a scrap for her, and well before I pick it up, she will trot to my side and stand, waiting. She must have read my mind. There's no other plausible explanation.

Everyone knows that Winston Churchill wrote formidable prose, but few are aware that he was a versatile versifier as well. When his daughter Mary's pug became ill, Churchill composed these lines for her:

> Oh, what is the matter with poor Puggy-wug?
> Pet him and kiss him and give him a hug.
> Run and fetch him a suitable drug,
> Wrap him up tenderly all in a rug,
> This is the way to cure Puggy-wug.

To his dog, every man is Napoleon; hence the constant popularity of dogs.

ALDOUS HUXLEY

A dog teaches a boy fidelity, perseverance, and to turn around three times before lying down.

ROBERT BENCHLEY

If you pick up a starving dog and make him prosperous, he will not bite you; that is the principal difference between a dog and a man.

MARK TWAIN

Drinking

(CONT'D)

A SUDDEN, VIOLENT JOLT of good corn liquor has been known to stop the victim's watch, snap his suspenders, and crack his glass eye right across.

IRVIN S. COBB

Malt does more than Milton can
To justify God's ways to man
Ale, man, ale's the stuff to drink
For fellows whom it hurts to think.

A. E. HOUSMAN

I'm only a beer teetotaler, not a champagne teetotaler.

GEORGE BERNARD SHAW

An alcoholic is someone you don't like who drinks as much as you do.

DYLAN THOMAS

They who drink beer will think beer.

WASHINGTON IRVING, *The Sketch Book*

When you ask a friend to dine,
Give him your best wine!
When you ask two,
The second best will do.

OLIVER WENDELL HOLMES

The warm, champagny, particular-old, brandy-punchy feeling.

IB.

When I played drunks, I had to remain sober because I didn't
know how to play them when I was drunk.

RICHARD BURTON

You couldn't have got that bottle away from him with a
stump puller.

Queen Victoria liked to "strengthen" her claret with whiskey.

The first drink before dinner is the Refresher;
The second is the Appetizer;
The third is the Rammer;
The fourth is the Infuriator.

H. S. REDMOND

Ann Landers's cure for hiccoughs: "I take a glass of water
and sip it very slowly, taking a deep breath after each sip."

After you have drunk one ounce of alcohol, you need one
hour to regain your full ability to drive.

The Gimlet cocktail—half gin, half Rose's lime juice—was
invented by a Royal Navy surgeon who was concerned that neat
gin impaired the efficiency of the officers in heavy weather. His
name was T. O. Gimlette.

The finest eye-opener on a frosty morning, and one that will
line your stomach all the rest of the day, is the Hot Brick, which

was brought to Virginia by a party of Kentucky foxhunters nearly a century ago. Here it is:

Bring to a boil: 1 cup sugar
1 cup butter
2 cups bourbon whiskey

Don't knock it until you've tried it!

An improbable legend says that the first champagne glass—the "saucer," not the "flute"—was molded from the breast of Marie Antoinette.

Prohibition Nostalgia

Bathtub gin ... bootleggers ... Izzy and Moe ... Mason jars ... Rum Row and rum runners ... rotgut ... Al Capone ... the Volstead Act ... speakeasies ... near-beer ... blind tigers ... Bevo ... moonshine ... corn likker ... "revenooers" ... the Eighteenth Amendment ... the St. Valentine's Day massacre ...

The ancient Greeks believed that wine drunk from an amethyst cup was nonintoxicating—which is what the word *amethyst* means.

My late friend Colonel Igor Moravsky speaking:

"Dose days, I am aide-de-comp to de Grond Dook. Vun night ve come to dis little inn, dip in Siberia, varry, varry cold! So ve sit up all night, drinking brondy to kip varm. Next morning de innkipper gifs me his bill, und I see 'Vun pint kerosene, two rubles'.

"I osk him, 'Vat is dis vun pint kerosene?'

"He say, 'My colonel, ven you ond de Grond Dook have drunk all de brondy in my poor house, you drink de kerosene from de lomp on de table.' "

Prof. Richard Porson, celebrated Greek scholar of the eighteenth century, was as famous for his intemperance as for his learning. It was not unusual for him to sit up for four successive days and nights, drinking steadily. When he challenged Horne Tooke, the philologist, to a duel, Tooke chose quarts of brandy as his weapon. The antagonists were halfway through the second quart when Porson went under the table.

Despite his brilliant editing of Greek texts, he is best remembered for this quatrain:

> I went to Frankfort and got drunk
> With that most learn'd professor, Brunck;
> I went to Worts, and got more drunken
> With that more learn'd professor, Ruhnken.

Eating
(CONT'D)

OSCAR WILDE to his waiter: "Tell the chef with my compliments that these are the very worst sandwiches in the whole world, and that when I ask for a watercress sandwich, I do not mean a loaf of bread with a field in the middle of it."

If the soup had been as warm as the wine, and the wine as old as the fish, and the fish as young as the maid, and the maid as willing as the hostess, it would have been a very good meal.

Anon.

The average Frenchman eats forty pounds of cheese a year, and he spends more time eating than does a man of any other nationality: two and three-quarter hours a day.

It has been said that no one can eat a quail a day for thirty consecutive days. Surfeit would set in.

A truly fastidious gourmet won't spread caviar with a knife made of anything but mother-of-pearl.

President Eisenhower's favorite dessert was prune whip. President Garfield's favorite dish was squirrel soup. President John Quincy Adams's was codfish pie.

"Diamond Jim" Brady had a Gargantuan appetite. When he died, restaurateur Charles Rector said, "I have lost my four best customers."

Caviar is to dining what a sable coat is to a girl in evening dress.

LUDWIG BEMELMANS

Gus Lobrano and I took Virginia Faulkner to lunch one day in July. (She wrote Polly Adler's autobiography, *A House is Not a Home.*) She told the waiter, "I'll begin with a half-dozen oysters, please." Then, seeing his look of dismay, she hurriedly added, "It's all right! I've got an 'R' in my name." Later, when we were having coffee, she thought she'd like to have a Martini. This time it was our turn to look dismayed. Virginia said, "What's the matter? Haven't you ever heard of an after-luncheon cocktail?"

John Hancock preferred to eat from pewter plates because they dulled the clatter of the table utensils, and the contents did not slide around. He had his manservants throw away his china service.

JOAN GATES

In ancient China, tea leaves were steamed, mashed into cakes, and steeped in hot salted water.

He was a bold man who first swallowed an oyster.

KING JAMES I

Everything you see, I owe to spaghetti.

SOPHIA LOREN

77

No man is lonely while eating spaghetti; it requires too much attention.

CHRISTOPHER MORLEY

Health food makes me sick.

CALVIN TRILLIN

Some years ago, I was flying from Tampa to Richmond, just after a snowstorm that had blanketed the whole southeast. As our plane circled to land at Atlanta, my seatmate nudged me and pointed to the white landscape: "One of their grits factories must have exploded," he said.

Jello tastes like running downhill with your mouth open.

A lady, Charlottesville, Virginia

Open letter to Emily Price Post, Amy Vanderbilt, "Miss Manners," and their sisters:

Dear Ladies: How does one consume onion soup without getting tangled in the strands of melted cheese, and having it stick to one's chin?

"We dined with the D——s last week. They had food enough for a dozen. Unhappily, we were sixteen. . . ."

N.B.

I clipped the following passage from the Travel Section of the Sunday *New York Times*, and did not realize until too late that I had not kept the writer's name or the date of the issue. I ask his/her forgiveness for the inadvertent piracy:

Roast young lamb is a favorite dish in Spain, and Spaniards argue over where it can be eaten at its best; how old should it be, 20 days or 28; is a forequarter more tender than a hindquarter; and if so, which forequarter, left or right? Some gourmets hold that lambs usually sleep on their right sides, so the left is the tenderer.

Some dieticians say that celery has "negative calories"—that is, eating a stalk of it consumes more calories than the stalk contains.

The Japanese believe that every new food they eat adds seventy-two days to their lives.

KENT CUSHMAN

The rat, when deep-fried in coconut oil, has the pleasing gaminess of squirrel or rabbit.

THOMAS Y. CANBY, *National Geographic*

Eccentrics
(CONT'D)

WE MIGHT DEFINE an eccentric as a man who is a law unto himself, and a crank as one who, having determined what the law is, insists on laying it down to others.

LOUIS KRONENBERGER

In the early 1900's, there was a section (2139) in the Code of Virginia which provided that the driver of a motor vehicle "shall keep a careful look ahead for the approach of horseback riders, [and] if requested by said rider, [such driver] shall lead the horse past the machine. Observance of this superannuated statute, it was John Armstrong Chaloner's ferocious pleasure to enforce. Armed with a revolver and shrouded in an Inverness cape, he would mount a horse, patrol the highway in front of The Merry Mills (his Virginia estate), summon motorists to a halt and demand to be led past. A green umbrella was riveted to the cantle of his saddle, a Klaxon to the pommel. After nightfall he hung port and starboard lanterns from the stirrups and what was literally a riding light from the girth. The Klaxon was his warning, the revolver his ultimatum. . . .

He believed that he was a silver box tarnished by magnetism, and that his stomach was a Leyden jar; and that he could change the color of his eyes at will.

J. BRYAN, III, "Johnny Jackanapes,"
The Virginia Magazine of History and Biography

So long as a man rides his hobby-horses peaceably and quietly, along the King's highway, and neither compels you or me to get up behind him—pray, Sir, what have either you or I to do with it?

LAURENCE STERNE

Charles VI of France (1368–1422) imagined that he was made of glass and would break if moved.

George Gould in a whimsical moment burned all the family books and records. This casual pyrotechnic gesture disposed, for the moment anyway, of the headaches implicit in well over half a billion dollars' worth of corporate and private resources.

LUCIUS BEEBE, *The Big Spenders*

Epitaphs
(CONT'D)

THIS ONE is less an epitaph than a memorial, but I want to include it because it is no longer on public view. It hung in the lobby of the Baltimore *Sun* building until recently, when it was taken down and stored. The *Sun* is dimmer for its removal:

HENRY LOUIS MENCKEN
1880 – 1956

NEWSPAPERMAN

AUTHOR   CRITIC

EDITOR   PHILOLOGIST

IF AFTER I DEPART THIS VALE
YOU EVER REMEMBER ME AND HAVE
THOUGHT TO PLEASE MY GHOST
FORGIVE SOME SINNER AND WINK
YOUR EYE AT SOME HOMELY GIRL

Epitaphs

Reading the epitaphs, our only salvation lies in resurrecting the dead and buring the living.

PAUL ELDRUGE

In lapidary inscriptions, a man is not upon oath.

DR. SAMUEL JOHNSON

I'm Smith of Stoke, aged sixty-odd,
I've lived without a dame
From youth-time on, and would to God
My dad had done the same.

THOMAS GARDY, *Epitaph on a Pessimist*

HERE LIES

MICHAEL ARLEN

AS USUAL

George S. Kaufman's: on himself,

OVER MY DEAD BODY.

and for a waiter:

BY AND BY,

GOD CAUGHT HIS EYE.

W. C. Fields: "On the whole, I'd rather be in Philadelphia."

King Arthur's:

HIC IACET ARTHURUS

REX QUONDAM ET FUTURUS

(Here lies Arthur, once and future king.)

Etiquette

ETIQUETTE is for the guidance of people who have no manners, as fashion is for those who have no taste.

QUEEN MARIE of Romania

At French dinner tables, the fork is laid with the points of the tines down, and the spoon with its tip down.

In most Eastern and Near Eastern countries, it is considered a shocking breach of etiquette to eat with one's left hand, which is reserved for an intimate utilitarian purpose.

If a Norwegian has invited you to dinner, it is obligatory for you to say "*Tak!*" ("Thank you!") to the hostess after each course. If a Swiss has invited you for seven o'clock, you are expected to ring his doorbell precisely then—not five minutes earlier or five minutes later. If a Bruxellois has invited you, you must bring your hostess flowers or chocolates, and you must refuse a second helping until she *beseeches* you to take it.

Table knives originally had pointed ends. Diners not only picked their teeth with them, but used them as weapons. Louis XIV therefore decreed that they should have rounded ends.

JOAN GATES

The original John Jacob Astor is said to have eaten his ice cream with a knife. Lord knows how or why!

IB.

In the late sixteenth century, napkins began to be tied around the neck for the protection of the large starched ruffs then in fashion—hence the expression, "making ends meet." A century later, men began wearing bibs to protect their clothing at meals. Somewhat later, women began wearing a lace or muslin "tucker" which they tucked into their décolletage on formal occasions—hence "to put on one's best bib and tucker."

Arthur Lee, the Member of Parliament who presented Chequers to the nation as a country residence for the Prime Minister, resigned from the fashionable Hurlingham Club in 1908 after his first visit. The flannel suit and Panama hat he thought appropriate for the hot summer afternoon had attracted unfriendly glances from his top-hatted and tail-coated fellow members.

KENNETH ROSE, *King George V*

Some very old-fashioned persons consider it vulgar to have portraits of women in the dining room.

Politeness: the most acceptable hypocrisy.

AMBROSE BIERCE

When your host carves a fowl and offers you your choice of "light meat or dark?" it's his nice-Nellie way of avoiding the indelicate "breast or leg?"

A Palm Beach dowager, observing that a newcomer, a young bride, was wearing a profusion of diamonds at a luncheon party, took her aside and told her, "My dear, one doesn't wear diamonds except in the evening."

"I thought so too," the girl said, "until I got them."

I have never dined at a private house in any of the Scandinavian capitals, so I can't vouch for the truth of something I was told about them: that next day you must send your hostess *an odd number* of flowers—seven or nine roses, say, but not six or eight. That's a strange one, isn't it?

Extremes
(CONT'D)

RACHEL CARSON, who wrote *Silent Spring* and *The Sea Around Us*, was such a conservator of life—*any* life—that when she dipped a small sample of water from the tidal flats in front of her house to put under her microscope, she always returned what was left when the examination was finished.

More than this, she returned it at the same tidal level that had obtained when she had dipped it, even though it meant that sometimes she had to set her alarm clock, put on slippers and bathrobe, and find her way down to the sea by flashlight.

CASKIE STINNETT

This, I think, is the Extreme Supreme.

No argument! The world's worst job is driving a school bus.

It blewed so hard, they was whitecaps on granmaw's pisspot.
Spring Hope, N.C.

My shoe soles were so thin, I could step on a dime and tell whether it was heads or tails.

He was so big, he could play tiddlywinks with manhole covers.

Last night I dined with David Cecil, who was so funny that I laughed the complexion off my face.

ELIZABETH LONGFORD, *The Pebbled Shore*

No more chance than a gasoline cat wearing kerosene pants in hell.

Anon.

A crewman said of the R.M.S. *Queen Mary*, "She could roll the milk out of a cup of tea."

Lincoln, to his cabinet, defending a large expenditure: "Gentlemen, you can't manure a ten-acre field with a fart."

The Snob Supreme

Charles Seymour (1662–1748), sixth Duke of Somerset, was known as the Proud Duke. That he thoroughly deserved the sobriquet is attested by the following anecdote, which Clifton Fadiman quotes from C. Roberts's *And So To Bath*:

The duke's first wife was Elizabeth, heiress to the great name and fortune of the Percys, dukes of Northumberland. When she

88

died in 1722, he married again; his second wife was Charlotte Finch, third daughter of the earl of Nottingham. Charlotte once made the mistake of tapping playfully on her husband's arm with her fan to attract his attention. He turned on her and said icily, "Madam, my first wife was a Percy, and *she* never took such a liberty."

Eyes
(CONT'D)

WITH AFFECTION beaming in one eye, and calculation out of the other.

CHARLES DICKENS

The human eye needs thirty seconds to adapt to a dark room.

STUART A. SANDOM, *Durations*

The medical name for those filmy shapes that slide across your eyeballs is *muscae volitantes*—"flying flies."

A lorgnette: A dirty look on a stick.

Anon.

The Israeli statesman Moshe Dayan wore a distinctive black patch over his blind eye. To the policeman who stopped him for speeding, Dayan argued, "I have only one eye. Which do you want me to watch, the speedometer or the road?"

If the ophthalmology business had not been so slow, Jules Stein would not have created the enormous entertainment conglomerate the Music Corporation of America; nor would Conan Doyle have written his immortal Sherlock Holmes stories.

The land turtle's humorous old eyes.

JOHN STEINBECK, *The Grapes of Wrath*

Whence the word "cataract"? It comes from the Latin *cataracta*, one of whose meanings is "a portcullis"—something that constitutes an obstruction. In the case of eye cataract, the obstruction is to light.

Faux Pas
(CONT'D)

Ambassador Joseph C. Grew was speaking at a Red Cross luncheon in Washington on the theme of selflessness. To illustrate it, he told how General Marshall, between an exhausting trip to China and an impending one to Europe, had taken time to address the Sunday meeting that had opened the Red Cross campaign, "although he had been looking forward," so Mr. Grew said, "to a weekend in the country with Mrs. Eisenhower."

The explosion of laughter woke Mr. Grew to his slip, which was made even more embarrassing by the presence of Mrs. Eisenhower herself. He begged her, "Please forgive me, and please make my apologies to the general."

She choked back her own laughter long enough to ask, "Which general?"

Don Carney, the host of a children's hour radio program in the 1930s, ended one of his broadcasts with an aside to an aide:

"There! That ought to hold the little bastards for another night!" His mike was "live."

My late friend Hugh Troy, the great practical joker and "master flabbergaster," told me this one:

His father, the professor of dairy science at Cornell, was being given a testimonial banquet, in honor of his election as president of the New York State Dairymen's League. Mrs. Troy was with him at the head table, so—Hugh said—there was no way she could miss the toastmaster's tribute to "Professor Troy, a man who chose a cow as his life's companion."

A few days after Pearl Harbor, the Chinese ambassador to Washington called on Frank Knox, the Secretary of the Navy. Mr. Knox, a sanguine soul, tried to hearten his despondent ally. He patted the ambassador's shoulder. "Don't you worry!" he said. "Don't worry for a minute! We're going to lick hell out of those yellow bastards!"

A Philadelphia couple gave an elegant dinner in honor of a visiting French countess. The cream of the Main Line was there, including a *grande dame* whose snobbishness had earned her the sobriquet "the Archduchess." Cocktails were served, accompanied by bits of toast unstably topped with egg and pimiento. When the company started in to dinner, the Archduchess noticed a small red blob on the countess's bodice and put out her hand to pluck it off, saying, "I'm afraid a scrap of pimiento—"

The countess drew back sharply. "By any chance," she asked, "are you referring to the ribbon of my *Légion d'Honneur?*"

Favorite Passages

TWENTY-TWO ACKNOWLEDGED CONCUBINES and a library of 62,000 volumes attested the variety of the Emperor Gordian's inclinations, and from the productions which he left behind him, it appears that the former as well as the latter were designed for use as well as for ostentation.

EDWARD GIBBON, *Decline and Fall of the Roman Empire*

The Duke of Wellington was asked what he considered the most injudicious exhortation ever delivered to troops. He said, "It was this one, spoken by a Portuguese commander on the eve of a battle in the Peninsular campaign: 'Men, whate'er befalls you on the morrow, never forget that you are Portuguese!' "

Note: "Portuguese" was then a contemptuous term for a poor soldier. But this anecdote is almost certainly a canard. It was not in Wellington's nature to tell such a cruel story, especially one about an ally.

94

Robert Benchley's favorite nursery rhyme:

> One, two, three,
> Buckle my shoe.

They laughed at Joan of Arc, but she went ahead and built it anyway.

GRACIE ALLEN

> Strong gongs groaning as the guns boom far,
> Don John of Austria is going to the war,
> Stiff flags straining in the night-blasts cold
> In the gloom black-purple, in the glint old-gold,
> Torchlight crimson on the copper kettle-drums,
> Then the tuckets, then the trumpets, then the cannon,
>   and he comes.
> Don John laughing in the brave beard curled,
> Spurning of his stirrups like the thrones of all the world,
> Holding his head up for a flag of all the free.
> Love-light of Spain—hurrah!
> Death-light of Africa!
> Don John of Austria
> Is riding to the sea.

G. K. CHESTERON, Lepanto

> There goes the hearse, the mourners cry,
> The respectable hearse goes slowly by....
> The fellow in the coffin led a life most foul,
> A fierce defender of the red bartender,
> At the church he would rail,
> At the preacher he would howl,
> He would trade engender for the red bartender,
> He would homage render to the red bartender,
> And in ultimate surrender to the red bartender
> He died of the tremens, as crazy as a loon,
> And his friends were glad, when the end came soon....
> And now, good friends, since you see how it sends ...
> The moral, the conclusion, the verdict now you know:
> The saloon must go! The saloon must go!

VACHEL LINDSAY, The Drunkard's Funeral

As recently as 1918, it was possible for a housewife... to march into a store with a five-cent piece, purchase a firkin of cocoa butter, a good secondhand copy of Bowditch, a hundredweight of quahogs, a shagreen spectacle case and sufficient nainsook for a corset cover, and emerge with enough left over to buy a balcony admission to *The Masqueraders*, with Guy Bates Post, and a box of maxixe.

S. J. PERELMAN, *The New Yorker*, October 29, 1979

That night came Arthur home, and while he climbed,
All in a death-dumb autumn-dripping gloom,
The stairway to the hall and looked and saw
The great Queen's bower was dark,—about his feet
A voice clung sobbing till he questioned it,
"What art thou?" and the voice about his feet
Sent up an answer, sobbing, "I am thy fool,
And I shall never make thee smile again."

ALFRED LORD TENNYSON, "The Last Tournament,"
Idylls of the King

There was a stir outside [General Lee's] tent, a moment of hesitation, and then someone brought in a bit of folded paper. It contained the brief and dreadful news [of Stonewall Jackson's death]. He had roused from his restless sleep and had struggled to speak. His mind had been wandering far—who knows how far?—but with an effort, in his even, low voice, he had said: "Let us pass over the river, and rest under the shade of the trees." And then, as so often on marches into the unknown, he had led the way.

DOUGLAS SOUTHALL FREEMAN, *R. E. Lee*

ROWAN: "Name an animal found only in Australia."
MARTIN: "A shark."
ROWAN: "No. It begins with a K."
MARTIN: "A kark."
ROWAN: "No. It ends with -aroo."
MARTIN: "A karkaroo."

Most of my other favorites are too long to quote here and too precious to abridge. They include the following:

The speech beginning "This day is call'd the feast of Crispin," in *Henry V*, Act iv, Scene 3.

Chapter 3, the "turtle chapter" in John Steinbeck's *The Grapes of Wrath*.

The story of Tamar, in II Samuel 13.

Chapter 8 of P. G. Wodehouse's *Leave It to Psmith*, in which Psmith escorts Eve Halliday around the grounds of Blandings Castle, and Chapter 17 of Wodehouse's *Right Ho, Jeeves*, in which Gussie Fink-Nottle, bulging with booze, awards the prizes at the Market Snodsbury Grammar School.

Golden stuff, all!

To move to a still larger scale: my favorite book is Kipling's *Kim*, and my least favorite book is *Freshman Chemistry*.

Flowers

An English geneticist, J. B. S. Haldane, has pointed out the relationship between the number of spinsters in a rural community and the number of snapdragons. Thus:

Spinsters like to keep cats; so, the more spinsters, the more cats. Cats kill mice; so, the more cats, the fewer mice. Mice raid beehives, so, the fewer mice, the more bees. Bees are the only insects heavy enough to weigh down the "lip" of a snapdragon and pollinate the flower; so, the more bees, the more snapdragons. Ergo, the more spinsters, the more snapdragons. Q. E. D.

One of the funniest men who ever wrote the English language was Donald Ogden Stewart (1894–1980), of Columbus, Ohio. If you can lay hands on any of his books, I beg you to do so. His own favorite among them was *Aunt Polly's Story of Mankind*. Mine is *Perfect Behavior*, a parody book of etiquette. I have borrowed the following paragraph from a chapter called "The Language of Flowers in Courtship":

As Miss Doe leaves the office you follow her, holding the potted geranium in your left hand. After a few paces you step up to her and offer the geranium, remarking, "I beg your pardon, miss, but didn't you drop this?" A great deal depends upon the manner in which you offer the plant and the way she receives it. If you hand it to her with the flower pointing upward, it means, "Dare I hope?" Reversed, it signifies, "Your petticoat shows about an inch, or an inch and a half." If she receives the plant in her right hand, it means, "I am"; left hand "You are," both hands—"He, she or it is." If, however, she takes the pot in both hands and breaks it on your head, the meaning is usually negative.

At the peak of the Tulip Mania, which raged through Holland in the 1630s, the whole country became infected. Nobles, citizens, farmers, mechanics, seamen, footmen, maidservants, even chimney-sweeps and old-clotheswomen, not only grew bulbs, but speculated in them. One bulb of an Admiral Liefkens cost the equivalent of about $750. A Viceroy was exchanged for "two loads of wheat, 4 loads of rye, 4 fat oxen, 8 fat swine, 12 fat sheep, 2 hogsheads of wine, 4 barrels of beer, 2 barrels of butter,

1,000 pounds of cheese, a complete bed, a suit of clothes, and a silver beaker"—a total price of $1,825. A Semper Augustus, white and red, tinted blue underneath, brought the record high: "a new and well-made carriage and two dappled-gray horses and accessories," plus enough cash to push the total up to more than $4,000.

Four thousand dollars for a single tulip bulb! Financial chaos followed, of course, but was the lesson learned? Listen: Almost exactly a century later, the Tulip Mania struck again, followed by chaos. And a century later, in 1836—you could look it up— it struck a *third* time. A new bulb, "Citadel of Antwerp" brought $3,120. The solid, stolid Dutch? Pah!

The hero of Dumas Père's *The Black Tulip* plants the bulb in April and sees it bloom in May. Ridiculous! Dumas knew more about plot than about bot. But in case you wonder what this imaginary flower might look like, here is the author's description: "The tulip was lovely, magnificent, superb, its stalk was more than eighteen inches high; it grew from the focus of four green leaves, slender and straight as lance shafts; and the whole of the flowers was as black and shining as jet."

If you have a flower garden that passing pickers find irresistible, *Punch* recommends posting this sign where trespassers can't miss it:

CAUTION! Taraxacum in These Beds

(*Taraxacum* is the dandelion.)

A sign I've always wanted to put at my gate is
PIANOS TUNED
(NO HOUSE CALLS)
but my wife wouldn't let me.

The American Beauty rose was discovered among an assortment of seedlings in the Newport gardens of George Bancroft, the seventeenth Secretary of the Navy. (Bancroft Hall at the Naval Academy was named for him.)

Oscar Wilde explained his look of fatigue one morning with "I was sitting up all night with a sick lily."

Sacheverell Sitwell describes a park at Estoril: "The massed geraniums ... are the color equivalent to a full brass band ... loud enough to drown a conversation."

I am now about to give you the most useless piece of information in this (or almost any other) book. Ready? The official flower of the Borough of Brooklyn, New York City, is the forsythia. Let me say it for you: A man must have the mind of a magpie to pick up and hoard a piece of trash like that!

E. J. APPLEWHITE

There are many ways to buttress your name against oblivion—to keep it alive after your death. One is to attach it to a prominent piece of landscape (Hudson's Bay, Mount Everest, Tasmania), or to a city (Washington, Leningrad, Melbourne). You might discover a disease (Alzheimer's, Parkinson's, Bright's) or become associated with some area of the human body (Eustachio, Fallopio, Langerhans), or you might achieve something important in physics or chemistry (Volta, Ohm, Watt). But surely the happiest way is through botany— the way chosen by Joel Poinsett, Caspar Wistar (*sic*), and Alexander Garden of America; J. G. Zinn and Anders Dahl of Sweden; Leonard Fuchs and J. F. von Eschscholtz (for whom a genus of poppies was named) of Germany; and William Forsyth of Great Britain.

This fragrant roster of sponsors-in-baptism does not include Billy Rose.

"Excellent herbs had our fathers of old. . . ." So begins one of Kipling's most charming poems. It goes on to list many of the herbs by their old-fashioned, rustic names: eyebright, call-me-to-you, rose of the run, and so on. Any elderly countrywoman could add a dozen more: love-lies-bleeding, Good-King-Henry, Jill-over-the-ground, kiss-me-quick (and its opposite, touch-me-not), Venus's looking-glass, Quaker-ladies, snow-in-summer, and so on. But I recently happened on the name of an herb that tops all: Welcome-home-husband-though-never-so-drunk. Did you ever?

101

The bucolic name for a dandelion is "pissabed." It's the same in French, too: *pissenlit*. I wonder how it originated.

Tulip bulbs have an unusual property, according to a Frenchman, one Dupinet, writing in 1563: "*Quand on voudra iouster avec les Dames, il est bon d'user de cette racine, car il rend l'homme gentil compagnon.*"

Or, "When you want to frolic with the girls, it's good to make use of this root, for it makes a man a pleasing companion."

Gems from the Silver Screen

[TONY CURTIS'S REAL NAME is Bernie Schwartz.] Universal Pictures appreciated Bernie's dark good looks and assigned him to *The Prince Who Was a Thief,* with Piper Laurie. The first words he uttered on the screen have since become a sort of classic. As this muscular young Arab prince takes the lovely Piper in his arms, he points beyond the camera and says, "Yonder lies da castle of my fadder da King."

SHELLEY WINTERS,
Condensed from *Shelley, Also Known as Shirley*

The second of my treasures is from the film *The Crusades,* starring Henry Wilcoxon as Richard the Lion-Hearted and Loretta Young as his Queen, Berengaria. The time is the night before Richard's attack on Jerusalem. Berengaria falls to her knees in front of him and begs, "Richard, you gotta capture Jerusalem tomorrow! You just gotta!"

103

It's a great line, worthy of standing beside Tony Curtis's, but the greatest I ever heard was in a Western. I can't remember the title, the star, or anything else about it except the one line itself, which was so magnificent it drove everything else out of my head. The scene is the prairie at night. The sheriff has unsaddled his faithful paint pony, Podnuh, and has gone to sleep, wrapped in his poncho. Presently we hear the sound of hoofbeats, distant but drawing nearer. Podnuh pricks up his ears, walks over to the sleeping sheriff, and nudges him with his muzzle. The sheriff sleeps on. Podnuh nudges him again. Now the sheriff awakes, sits up, and stares straight into the camera. " 'Pears," he says, " 'pears like the critter wants to tell me suthin'!"

Max Reinhardt was famous for the perfection of detail in his pictures. Every trifle had to be *just so*. Before the première of his *A Midsummer Night's Dream*, he distributed stills to the press. One showed a posed group of the cast in Grecian costume, and we were amused to notice—there in the very front row—a small black boy wearing sneakers.

In the opening scene of *Casablanca*, Rick's Café Americain is located next to the airport; later, it is in the center of town.

Audiences in college towns feel few restrictions when it comes to commenting on plots or performers. In the Princeton of my youth, we used to frequent the Arcade Theatre as much for the "asides" as for the professional entertainment. I remember a romantic film in which a mother cat strolled across the screen, followed by a file of seven kittens. Someone greeted her with a singsong, "Oh—I know—what—*you've*—been—doing!"

The most memorable comments were, of course, the bawdy ones. John Gilbert was breathing down Garbo's neck, pausing only to nibble her ear. "Come with me," the subtitle read, "and life will be a bed of roses. . . ." This brought a warning from the audience: "Look out, lady! There may be a prick in those roses!"

Navy audiences were even bawdier. One evening on the carrier *Lexington*, the film opened on a view of a long flight of steps, with a girl tap-dancing down toward the camera. When she reached the foot, she leaped high into the air and came down in a spreadeagled split. "No!" cried hundreds of voices. "NO! Save it, *save it*!"

One more shipboard-movie comment. I heard this one on the battleship *Massachusetts*, when she finally came to anchor in Havannah Harbor, Efate, in the New Hebrides (now Vanuatu), after weeks of aimless cruising around the southwest Pacific. The word was passed that we'd celebrate with movies that night, and a screen was rigged on the fantail, almost under the muzzles of the 16-inch guns in Number 3 turret. Long before darkness fell and the boatswain had piped "Let's go to the movies!" the crew had crowded onto the after deck, whistling and stamping and wolf-calling. Half of us were yelling for a Betty Grable picture, the other half for an Ava Gardner. And what did we get? An insipid juvenile, *Andy Hardy, Editor*. It opened to a chorus of groans and had been running for a couple of purposeless minutes when a crisp voice barked, "Number Three turret, *fire*!"

One of the most unforgettably vivid sequences in any movie was Gene Kelly's night-time dance in *Singin' in the Rain*. The clarity of the raindrops was achieved by the use of milk instead of water.

NORMAN HICKMAN

For all the painstaking work that goes into a moving picture, for all the thrills and laughs and heart throbs that it brings us, and for all its claims to be High Art, the wagon wheels still turn backward.

A Gentleman —
(CONT'D)

—CAN PLAY THE BAGPIPES, but doesn't.

I can make a lord, but only God Almighty can make a gentleman.

KING JAMES I of England

He is every other inch a gentleman.

REBECCA WEST

It is at unimportant moments that a man is a gentleman. At important moments, he ought to be something better.

G. K. CHESTERTON

A Gentleman—

Geography

SHANGRI-LA IS, of course, the scene of James Hilton's novel *Lost Horizon*. Ruritania is the imaginary kingdom in Anthony Hope's romances, *The Prizoner of Zenda* and its sequel, *Rupert of Hentzau*. Gulliver traveled to Laputa and Brobdingnag and other lands that existed only in Jonathan Swift's mind. Cockaigne and the Big Rock Candy Mountain are imaginary places of idleness and luxury. Old seamen and cavalrymen look forward to Fiddler's Green, where every amenity is bigger and better than anywhere else. There are dozens, scores, of these places, some mythical, some legendary, some fictional: Never-Never-Land, Poictesme, Erewhon (an anagram for Nowhere), Utopia (Greek for No Place), Valhalla, Nirvana, Paradise, Heaven. The lands of immortality aside, the best known of them in the English-speaking world is probably Oz, the seat of the Wonderful Wizard. Where do you think its creator, L. Frank Baum, found its name? On the O–Z drawer of his filing cabinet.

Which is the world's highest continent? Antarctica, which has an average altitude of over 6,000 feet.

And what is Wallace's Line? An imaginary line, devised by naturalist Alfred Russel Wallace, dividing the animal life of the Australian region from that of the Asiatic region. It runs east of the Philippines and through the middle of Indonesia—between Borneo and Celebes, Bali and Lombok.

Louisville, Kentucky, is closer to Windsor, Ontario, than to Memphis, Tennessee; Lee County, Virginia, is closer to the capitals of six other states than to Richmond, the capital of Virginia.

A billboard at one of the entrances to Knoxville, Tennessee, proudly announces its claim to be "America's 77th largest city."

E. J. APPLEWHITE

You can get frostbite on the Equator—yes, if you happen to be standing on the icy slopes of Mount Kenya.

Latitude 0 and longitude 0 is a point in the Atlantic Ocean about 700 miles south of Ghana.

Gobi means "desert" in Mongolian. *Sahara* means "desert" in Arabic. *Nyanza* means "lake" in Bantu. So when we speak of the Gobi Desert, etc. . . .

Can you identify Gondwanaland? It was a large land mass which broke up and drifted apart millions of years ago. It now forms part of South America, Africa, India, Antarctica, and West Australia.

Brazil is the only country named for a tree. When Portuguese explorers arrived there in the sixteenth century, they found a tree whose wood was as reddish as live coals (*brasa*). They called it *brasil* and exported it as dyewood. Soon the country was known by the name of this valuable tree, called in English Brazilwood.

Q. Name the southernmost, northernmost, westernmost and easternmost states of the U.S.

A. Hawaii is the southernmost, Alaska is all the rest. (The hemispheric division goes through the western Aleutian Islands.)

Suwannee, as in the Suwanee River, is a corruption of its original name, "San Juan."

The Great War

WHEN THE STORM of the Great War of 1914–18 blew itself out, it left my fourteen-year-old memory littered with fragments—words and phrases—like the rusting barbed wire and landing craft that World War II left on the beaches of Normandy. Hearing or reading one of those fragments even now, seventy-odd years later, re-creates the Great War for me. Everyone who lived then has his own cabinet of souvenirs. Here are some of mine:

Sarajevo ... "A scrap of paper" ... no-man's-land ... Zeppelins ... Nurse Edith Cavell ... *Kultur* ... Sam Browne belts ... The Beast of Berlin ... Bleeding Belgium ... Tommies ... *Minenwerfer* ... cooties ... Chasseurs Alpins ... The Red Baron ... buddies ... "I have a rendezvous with Death at some disputed barricade" ... Big Bertha ... *Schrecklichkeit* ... "The Better 'Ole" ... Uhlans ... "The ladies from Hell" ... "The Hun" ... Fokkers and Spads and Sopwith Camels ... Mata Hari ... *Pick-*

elhaube ... "Devil Dogs" ... the French 75 ... puttees ... "In Flanders fields the poppies blow/ Between the crosses, row on row" ... The Boche ... Blighty ... *Me und Gott* and *Gott mit Uns* ... "Going West" ... poilus ... Raemakers' cartoons ... Sergeant York ... "Uncle Sam Wants YOU!"

The songs of that war are far more powerful stimuli to memory than these bits and pieces. I find I can recall a dozen of them:

Over There
There's a Long, Long Trail
How Ya Gonna Keep 'Em Down on the Farm?
Madelon
Keep the Home-Fires Burning
Hello, Central, Give Me No Man's Land
Pack Up Your Troubles in Your Old Kit Bag
Goodbye, Broadway, Hello, France!
We'll Hang Out Our Washing on the Siegfried Line
Roses of Picardy
Good Morning, Mr. Zip-Zip-Zip
My Buddy
Oh, How I Hate to Get Up in the Morning
The Rose of No Man's Land
Goodbye Paw! Goodbye, Maw!

I nearly forgot to list two of the most popular of them all: "Mademoiselle from Armentieres" and "Tipperary."

I mentioned Uhlans some lines ago. The word brings up an especially vivid memory: At the end of 1927, I was staying on a coffee plantation at Ngong, in Kenya. My host was a New Zealander, Ronald Bruce-Smith, a lieutenant-colonel retired from a lancer regiment. We were swimming one day when my eyes were caught by a thick, jagged scar that ran from inside his right elbow—his lance arm—up into his armpit. I had to ask about it, of course. Well, Ronnie's regiment had been among the first to see action in France. There, one afternoon, they surprised a squadron of Uhlans—also a crack lancer regiment—and engaged them, lance to lance. That was when Ronnie took the wound that left the scar.

Would you have bet that Europeans fought with lances as recently as 1914? I also know a pilot, an Australian, who had a spear thrown through the wing of his plane, in flight.

Ronnie, in turn, brings to mind Count Mippipopolous, and *his* scars, in Hemingway's *The Sun Also Rises*. He is drinking champagne with Jake and Brett, and remarks,

"I have been around a very great deal.... I have been in seven wars and four revolutions.... I have got arrow wounds. Have you ever seen arrow wounds?"...

The count stood up, unbuttoned his vest, and opened his shirt.... Below the line where his ribs stopped were two raised white welts. "See on the back where they come out." Above the small of the back were the same two scars, raised as thick as a finger....

"Where did you get these?" I asked.

"In Abyssinia, when I was twenty-one years old."

The count had indeed "been around a very great deal."

Gavrilo Princip, the Serbian nationalist who murdered Archduke Franz Ferdinand of Austria and his wife in Sarajevo in 1914, thereby igniting the Great War, is the only assassin to have a memorial erected in his honor. A commemorative plaque on the wall of the Young Bosnia Museum in Sarajevo marks the site of the momentous shooting.

Hair

Barber: "How do you like your hair cut, sir?"
   Groucho Marx: "In silence."

Some fifty to sixty hairs fall from the normal, healthy human scalp every twenty-four hours. Hair grows about an inch a month. A plucked-out hair will grow back in about a month. Some hair continues growing for six years after death. Hair grows about twenty-five feet in a lifetime.

Delilah didn't cut or shave Samson's hair. Judges 16:19 says that "she made him sleep upon her knees; and she called for a man, and she caused him to shave off the seven locks of his hair; and she began to afflict him and his strength went from him."

Barber: "How do you like your hair cut, sir?"
   Winston Churchill: "In silence."

Legend says that Marie Antoinette's hair turned white over-night. Perhaps it actually did. But it's a fact that the hair of my late cousin, Alfred Wither, turned *black* overnight—the night in 1917 before he went to enlist in the U.S. Army. I don't know how old he was then; he must have been in his fifties, because he had served in the Queen's Royal Rifles in the Sudan Campaign of the early 1880s. (I've seen his medal, with its dark blue ribbon.) The army accepted him; he began training, and he got away with it until his hair dye began to wear off at a time and place where no more was available. His graying hair soon betrayed him, and out he went.

Harold Ross, the late editor of *The New Yorker*, wore his hair in a thick, bushy pompadour. The lovely Ina Claire, seeing it for the first time, burst out, "Oh, to walk through it barefooted!"

Barber: "How do you like your hair cut, sir?"
Yul Brynner: "In silence."

Peter the Great's program to westernize his empire included a discouraging tax on beard and mustaches, in the belief that most western men were clean-shaven. You could keep your beard if you paid a special beard tax.

If you live in a community where deer browse in your foliage, ask your barber to give you an envelope of sweepings from around his chair. Put a few pinches of hair into small porous bags (like Bull Durham sacks), and the human scent will keep the deer away.

Barbers tell me that for a clean, smooth shave, you should rub your beard with water as hot as you can stand it, wait three minutes, rub it again, then lather up and shave. It works for me.

When King George IV of England died, there were found in one of his cabinets more than a hundred locks of women's hair. Some of these were still plastered with powder and pomatum. Some were mere little golden curls, such as grow low down on a girl's neck; others were streaked with gray. . . . I have been privileged to look at all these locks and I have seen a *clairvoyante* take them one by one and, pinching them between her little fingers, tell of the love that each symbolized . . . of a boudoir hung with green-grass satin, and a tryst at Windsor; of one who, in her great simplicity, thought her child would one day be King of England; of an arch-duchess with blue eyes, and a silly little flautist from Portugal; of women that were wantons and fought for his favour; great ladies that he loved dearly; girls that gave themselves to him humbly.

MAX BEERBOHM, *King George the Fourth*, condensed

Barber: "How do you like your hair cut, Sir?"
George Washington: "In silence."

He had the widest, blackest, an' best-groomed an' longest beard I've ever seen off'n a yak.

KIN HUBBARD

Miss Fern Barlow has left her job at the Bon Ton Shoppe so's she can devote all her time to her hair.

IB.

I hadn't realized that so many hair styles were named for persons who had sponsored them. For instance, the Pompadour (1721–64), the Imperial (Emperor Napoleon III, 1808–73), Burnsides or Sideburns (General Ambrose Burnside, 1824–81), Dundrearys (Lord Dundreary in *Our American Cousin*, 1858), and of course, the Psyche knot, and the Madonna style as featured by the Duchess of Windsor.

Overheard at a Navy party in Honolulu, 1944, a jealous Navy wife to another Navy wife: "Back off from my husband, or I'll pull your Navy-gold hair out by its Navy-blue roots!"

King Louis XII of France was unable to grow a beard.

> How many cowards, whose hearts are all as false
> As stairs of sand, wear yet upon their chins
> The beards of Hercules and frowning Mars;
> Who, inward search'd, have livers white as milk.
>
> SHAKESPEARE, *The Merchant of Venice*

The Human Body

THE LARGEST ORGAN is the skin.

The appendix, the navel, and the nipples on a man's breast are utterly useless; they have no known function at all.

In addition to the processes of breathing, circulation, and digestion, the involuntary actions of the body include winking.

There are 60,000 miles of blood vessels in the body and about 100 square meters of lung tissue.

My late friend David Salinger used to say that he suffered from "Salinger's disease." It was characterized by extreme lassitude, but there were no other symptoms, the patient being too indolent to show any.

Alexander the Great's body smelled of violets.

The average person's left foot is a trifle larger than the right.

A few years ago in Europe, there was sold at auction a shriveled morsel of flesh represented as Napoleon's penis. How it was authenticated, and who bought it, and why and for how much, I did not inquire.

The mitral valve is so called because it is shaped like a bishop's mitre. A muscle is so called because the movements of certain of them resemble those of a little mouse, or *musculus*, under the skin.

It was not until I attended a few postmortems that I realized that even the ugliest exteriors may contain the most beautiful viscera, and was able to console myself for the facial drabness of my neighbors in omnibuses by dissecting them in my imagination.

J. B. S. HALDANE

The toxin of *Bacillus botulinus* is the most poisonous of all known substances when taken by the mouth. About six pounds of it would probably be sufficient to kill the entire human race.

IB.

The jaw muscle is the most powerful one in the body.

The last faculty a dying person loses is generally the hearing. Be careful what you say at a deathbed!

A registered nurse

An attractive lady of my acquaintance developed a small growth next to a corner of her mouth, and her dermatologist recommended that she let him remove it. When she agreed, he added, "You'll need a small graft to avoid a scar. Where shall I take it from?" The lady slapped her buttocks. "Right here!," she said. "Then, when someone I don't like kisses me, I'll laugh to myself and think what he's really kissing!"

Two thousand cells of the human body, side by side, would cover about one square inch; one of them alone could hold more than 60 million polio viruses.

"Duels at dawn" have a rational explanation: Abdominal wounds are harder to treat if the victim has recently eaten. At dawn, both duelists' stomachs are probably empty.

On the remote chance that you may find it hard to remember the order of nerves entering the superior optical tissues on the skull behind the eyes, a convenient mnemonic is: Lazy French Tarts Sit Naked In Anticipation—Lateral, Frontal, Trochlear, Superior branch of motor nerve, Nasociliary, Inferior branch of ocular motor nerve, Abduct.

Catherine de Medici's waist is said to have been only 13 inches around.

Some parts of the body—e.g., the foot, the bottom—enjoy (or blush under) a variety of nicknames or slang names, but none more than the head. Here are a baker's dozen of synonyms that come readily to mind:

Noggin, nut, sconce, nob (knob), pate, bean, poll, belfry, bun, skull, dome, coco, noddle.

Information, Please

WHAT IS THE DERIVATION of the word "rubber" as used in such games as bridge, cribbage, and backgammon? No one seems to know, not even the magisterial *Oxford English Dictionary*, though "rubber" has been used in that sense since at least 1599.

How many people do you know who live in the house they were born in?

Why is it that when we idly glance at a clock or wristwatch, we so often see that its hands stand precisely at 12? Does some psychic signal-gun fire then? Or what is it?

What has become of all the fifty-cent pieces?

What did God have in mind when He created hiccoughs?

Gold is more precious than silver, isn't it? Then why does a second lieutenant wear gold insignia and a first lieutenant silver, instead of vice versa? The same for a Navy lieutenant j.g. and an ensign, a commander and a lieutenant commander, a lieutenant colonel and a major.

Why do private eyes (in TV shows and movies) never button their shirt collars? When they come into a client's house, why don't they ever take off their hats? And when they go into his (the client's) office, why do they always perch on the edge of a desk?

What could have inspired someone to string a cat's intestines on a frame, and scrape a tune with hairs from a horse's tail?

What is the meaning of the suffix *-ington*, as in Washington, Carrington, Torrington, etc?

Which one of the large and prominent Katz family discovered and christened the Catskill Mountains?

Why do so many TV panelists wear neckties of the same brownish-red?

Will someone please explain centripetal force to me?

Why can't American taxis be clean, roomy, and comfortable like English taxis?

When did men start parting their hair?

"He fell in love with a dimple, but made the mistake of marrying the whole girl." Who made this wonderful remark? Was it George Ade? Abe Martin? Ambrose Bierce? I hope some reader will tell me.

When was the last time there was no airplane in the skies anywhere?

Has any important invention or discovery ever come from the southern hemisphere?

123

A fire engine, an ambulance, a mail truck, and a police patrol wagon are converging on a crossroads at full speed and from different directions. Which has the legal right of way? I've been told it is the mail truck, but I don't know.

When did the use of middle names become popular? I note Charles James Fox (1749–1806), Richard Brinsley Sheridan (1751–1816), John Quincy Adams (1767–1848).

Have there ever been any girl prodigies? Any little Miss Mozarts? STOP PRESS! I have just read about a twelve-year-old Hungarian girl who is expected to be acclaimed as an international master at chess by the time this is printed. Bobby Fischer didn't achieve this eminence until he was fourteen.

Inglisch Spocken
Here

FOLLOWING IS A COLLECTION of notices in what was intended to be English. Some of the items are my own happy discoveries. Some were sent me by traveling friends. Some I have pilfered from other collections. As I read the lot, I can only pray that our native language will survive the Berlitzkrieg.

A butcher in Nahariyya, Israel: "I slaughter myself twice daily."

A barber in Tokyo: "All customers promptly executed."

A clothier in Brussels: "Mourning and sportswear."

One in Budapest: "Very smart! Almost pansy!"

And one in Paris: "Dresses for street walking."

A restaurant in Algeciras: "Revolting eggs." (This is a literal translation of *huevos revueltos*, scrambled eggs.)

A barber in Zanzibar: "Gentlemen's throats cut with nice sharp razors."

A hotel in Torremolinos: "We highly recommend the hotel tart."

125

Another Spanish hotel, location not identified: "The provisions of a large French widow in every apartment adds to the visitor's amenities."

A hotel in Tokyo: "Is forbidden to steal towels, please. If you are not person to do such, please not to read notice."

Hotel Washington, Colón: "Because of the impropriety of entertaining persons of the opposite sex in the bedroom, it is requested that the lobby be used for this purpose."

Rex Hotel, Havana: "Guests are prohibited from walking around in the lobby in large groups in the nude."

A hotel in Saigon: "If any other person makes use of the room, *she* must also register, whatever the length of *her* stay." (My italics.)

The Fujia Hotel, Miyanoshita, Japan: "We now have a Sukiyaki Restaurant with lodging facilities for those who want have experiences on Japanese bedding."

A Tokyo hotel has this notice on its elevator doors: "Do Not Open Door Until Door Opens First."

Slavija Hotel, Belgrade: "Let us know about any inficiency as well as leaking on the service."

A hotel in Athens: "Visitors are expected to complain at the office from 9 to 11 A.M. daily."

Hotel Deutschland, Leipzig: "Do not enter the lift backwards and only when lit up."

A hotel in Bucharest: "The lift is being fixed for the next four days. During this time you will be unbearable."

Hotel del Paseo, Mexico City: "We sorry to advise you that by a electric desperfect in the generator master of the elevator we have the necessity that don't give service at our distinguishable guests."

In the window of a travel agency in Barcelona: "Go away."

A hotel in Moscow: "If this is your first visit to the U.S.S.R., you are welcome to it."

A hospital in Barcelona: "Visitors two to a bed and half an hour only."

A Paris hotel: "A sports jacket may be worn to dinner, but not trousers."

Same hotel: "Tea in a bag just like mother."

A hotel on the Gaspé Peninsula: "No dancing in the bathrooms!" (The friend who sent me that one added, "Spoiled my plans for the evening.")

Notice on a *wagon-lit* in India: "Do not invite thieves to sleep on the floor."

In Durban, Natal: "Bare feet and dogs not allowed in escalator."

At the entrance to the Seville cathedral: "It is forbidden to enter a woman even a foreigner if dressed as a man."

A dance hall in a London suburb, spotted by W. W. Pett Ridge nearly a century ago: "The directors have the right to refuse admission to any lady they think proper."

A notice on every table in the dining room of a hotel in Columbo, Sri Lanka: "All vegetables in this establishment have been washed in water especially passed by the management." (I consider that a prize specimen.)

The Restaurant des Artistes, Montmartre: "We serve five o'clock tea at all hours."

A bakery, Vale of Kashmir: "First-class English loafer."

The Grand Palais Hotel, Ostend, issues to players on its miniature golf course a card of "recommandations." Number 2 requests them to "level with the feet holes or mound do by playing on the game." I take this to mean "Please replace divots," but Number 4 eludes me completely: "No working players are invited to stay on the stony mat." Well?

127

Hotel Principe Alfonso, Palma de Mallorca: "Every Sunday very great kocks fights at Ca'n Veta jurt in front of the ancient rase horses."

Palma also offers the tourist a leaflet advertising the Caves of Arta, and commending their "suporizing infinity of graceful columns of 21 meter and by downward, wich prives the spectator of all anaimexion and plunges in dumbness."

A final gem from Palma. Robert Graves found this one on a shop window: "This is a lechery of confidence." (*Lechería* is the Spanish for "dairy.")

Malcolm Bradbury of *Punch* copied off for me a cabin-door notice on the Spanish ship carrying him to the Canary Islands: "Help savering apparata. In emergins behold many whistles! Associate the stringing apparata about the bosoms and meet behind. Flee then to the indifferent lifesaveringshippen obediencing the instructs of the vessel!"

Still, such nonsense isn't wholly so; you can skim a gist of sorts from the wildly boiling words. But here is the tag I saw on a lamp for sale in Estoril, and none of us has yet determined whether it is instructive, descriptive, or historical:

"The present lamp is a reply of the used's in almost every's the province from Portugal, among the century XVII–XIX even a usage in some recondite's and old village's. Wholesome to illumination to middle by oil; the that empty of & deposit, and immediately kindle the wick's. The pincer, bucket, etc., from some, sound towards clean the wick's of the burning."

A dentist in Hong Kong: "Teeth extracted by latest methodists."

Another elevator sign, this from Tokyo: "Keep your hands away from unnecessary buttons for you."

I once stayed at a hotel in Brisbane, Australia, where the elevators had this helpful sign: "If you wish to go up, press the button marked 'up.' If you wish to go down, press the button marked 'down.'"

128

Invitation in a bedroom in the Hotel California, Rio de Janeiro: "Visit the hairdresser in the Sub Soil of this Hotel."

E. Howard Hunt sent me this one from a hole-in-the-wall restaurant in Mexico City: "U.S. Hots Dog."

Instructions accompanying an alarm clock bought in Hong Kong: "To set alarm set alarm hand to time desired to wake. To change time desired to wake, reset alarm to the time desired to."

At the entrance to a hotel swimming pool on the French Riviera: "Swimming is forbidden in the absence of the savior." And on a pool in Columbo, Sri Lanka: "Do not use the diving board when the swimming pool is empty."

And finally, my favorite. I quote it from *The Motorist's Weekend Book*, whose editor says only that "it is an extract from 'regulations' for a foreign [motoring] event, kindly translated by the organizers for the benefit of English entrants." Here it is, and it's a lulu:

"Competitors will defile themselves on the promenade at 11 A.M., and each car will have two drivers who will relieve themselves at each other's conveniences."

I'd happily contribute to a purse for the heaven-inspired innocent who composed that marvelous sentence, if he'd promise to keep on writing and never to open an English dictionary.

Inventions

(CONT'D)

A DENTIST, DR. WILLIAM I. DISMUKES, invented the folding bed. Another dentist, Dr. Samuel Greif, invented a "Device for Writing the Oriental Languages on Occidental Typewriting Machines and Vice Versa." (I don't believe it's possible! When Dr. Greif made this announcement, I'll bet he had his tongue in his cheek, wedged down with billets of cotton wool.)

Still another dentist, Dr. C. C. Carroon, invented a process for casting aluminum. Thanks to it, contractors were able to put an aluminum tip on the Washington Monument, a problem which had hitherto baffled them. There is no evidence that any professional inventor practiced dentistry as a sideline.

Who invented the alarm clock? Leonardo de Vinci. His alarm clock woke the sleeper by gently rubbing his feet.

HY GARDNER

Thomas A. Edison has more than a thousand inventions to his credit. Here is the story, hitherto unpublished, of how he perfected one of them:

The scene is his laboratory, late on a night in October 1879. He is bent over his workbench, trying to fit a sort of plug into an orifice in a glass bulb. There is a knock at the door. He does not look up. Another knock. At last Edison calls impatiently, "Well, what is it?" Mrs. Edison enters. "Tom, dear," she says, "it's almost two o'clock. You'll ruin your health if you don't get some sleep!" He sighs. "I'm sorry, Mary. I didn't realize the time. I'm right on the edge of something big. Give me an hour more, and I'll turn in. I promise!"

She tiptoes out. Edison reshapes the plug and twists it a trifle, and again and again, and presently it slips smoothly into the orifice. "There!" he says aloud. "Got it!" He attaches two wires to the base of the plug and holds the bulb to his ear. Nervously he throws a small switch. "Hello?" he says. "Hello?"

(Forgive me for dragging in this Shaggy Dog story. I did so because it seems to fit, and because I think it's funny.)

Here is a case of invention by accident:

In 1838 Francis Pettit Smith (later Sir Francis) tested his 237-ton, steam-driven [ship] *Archimedes*—fittingly named, because it was to be propelled by a screw with two convolutions [turns], luckily made of wood. The first trial met the Admiralty's requirement, a 4- to 5-knot speed. But the vessel collided with a floating bottle, which broke off one of the convolutions. Smith, though in despair, started his engine again, and this time, with a single convolution, the *Archimedes* raced forward at 9 knots, as much as the best paddle steamers could do with incomparably more powerful machinery.

EGON LARSEN, *Inventors' Cavalcade*

Irritants
(CONT'D)

LINES I NEVER WANT to hear or read again:

—who requested that he not be identified.
—batteries not included.
—some assembly required.
—That's a good question.
—Please feel free to contact us.
—after these important commercial announcements.
—said in a television interview.
—plus postage and handling.
—investigative reporter.
—That's what it's all about.
—Postmaster: deliver only to addressee.
—Personal and confidential.
—Will you give me a raincheck on that?
—for a limited time only.
—We'll play it by ear.

—Pending notifcation of next of kin.

—We will pause now for these important messages.

—alive and well and living in . . .

—the length and breadth of this great nation.

The sudden realization that there's no one left from whom you may expect to inherit.

Waiting, especially in a doctor's or dentist's waiting room.

The discovery that you have neglected to fill in a stub in your checkbook, and have no recollection of the payee or the amount.

Having your telephone stop ringing just as you pick it up.

Clip-on coathangers in hotel closets, silently implying that the guest is a thief.

Letters beginning "Frankly—"

People who crowd into an elevator while the passengers are still trying to get out.

Waiters and waitresses who tell you their names.

Wives who interrupt their husbands to say, "No, darling, it wasn't a Tuesday; it was a Wednesday—now go ahead with your story."

Clowns in the background of a TV news film who lean into the camera and make faces and wiggle their fingers in their ears.

Members of the audience who start applauding a tap-dancer (and thereby drown out his taps) when he is only partway through his act.

Drivers who park in part of the neighboring space.

Persons who telephone you and start a conversation without first identifying themselves.

Strangers who write you for information, but don't enclose a stamped envelope.

Idiots who call you early in the morning and ask in astonishment, "Oh, did I wake you?"

And those who speak of "daylight saving*s* time" and those who pronounce "consul" as if it were spelled "counsel."

Vogue words and phrases, such as *gutsy, syndrome, state of the art, meaningful, address* (as in "I shall address this subject more fully later"), *relevance, foreseeable future, scenario, a metaphor for, exclusive, at this point in time, collectibles, -athon* (as in *walkathon, talkathon, telethon*), *empathy, fun people, host* (as in "they hosted a party"), *flight attendant* for *stewardess*, and all other such pretentiousness. *Pilot error, the cutting edge, thrust* (as in "the thrust of his argument"), *software, zesty and crunchy, ball-park figure* (meaning a rough estimate in round numbers, whereas real ball-park figures are exact: "Attendance today is 31,449"), a *4-litre car* (is that good or bad, big or little?—it means nothing to me), *fight* (as in "Fight tooth decay! and "Fight that lazy colon"), *massive* (as in *stroke, retaliation, cost overrun*), *courtesy phone, Operation* ———, *task force* (for a committee), *workshop* (for an office), *y'know . . . y'know . . . y'know . . .*

Modern packaging, which requires an ax and a blowtorch to open the box or envelope—e.g., the salted nuts they give you on airplanes.

Men's new haberdashery, ambushed with invisible pine.

Postmarks so faint or so smeared that you can't decipher them.

Those small sheets of cardboard stapled into your magazine.

Solicitation by telephone.

TV commercials that end, "Call one-eight-hundred, five-five-five, five-six-seven-eight. That is, one-eight-hundred, five-five-five, five-six-seven-eight. I repeat: one-eight-hundred, five-five-five, five-six-seven-eight."

Ads that are sticky with "only" and "just" (as in "Only $218,000" or "Just $17,000").

Languages
(CONT'D)

IF YOU SEE THIS SIGN, ATUM BOM, in a fishmonger's window in Portugal, don't be alarmed. It means "good tuna."

The French word *après-midi*, "afternoon," may be either masculine or feminine.

The more one talks about Latin, the easier it is to see why the Roman Empire fell.

LORD DERBY

We know that a "drawing room" was originally a "withdrawing room," and that a "parlor" is a place to *parler*—talk. But what is a boudoir? It's a place to pout—*bouder*.

The second largest French-speaking city in the world? Montreal.

English and French words are stuffed with silent letters
(through, Wednesday; vous, Menthe), but every letter in a Spanish word is pronounced.

Last Words
(CONT'D)

ANNE BOLEYN: "The executioner is, I believe, very expert, and my neck is very slender."

James Buchanan Duke, founder of the American Tobacco Company, told his only child, Doris, "Take care of our money!'"

Gertrude Stein: "Well, what is the answer?" And after a long pause, "But what, then, is the question?"

Disraeli, in reply to the suggestion that Queen Victoria come to his deathbed: "Why should I see her? She will only want me to give a message to Albert."

Henry James: "So here it is at last, the distinguished thing."

Viscountess Astor, to her children gathered at her deathbed: "Am I dying, or is this my birthday?"

Erskine Childers, an Irish patriot condemned to the firing squad: "Take a step or two forwards, lads, it will be easier that way." (Childers was the author of one of the first good spy novels, *The Riddle of the Sands*.)

Lord Holland, on his deathbed, referring to George Selwyn, a friend who was morbidly fascinated by death and corpses: "If he calls again, show him up. If I am alive, I shall be delighted to see him. If I am dead, he will be glad to see me."

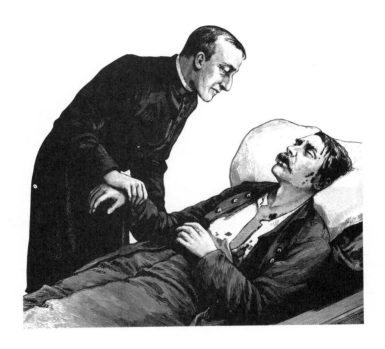

Anna Pavlova: "Get my swan costume ready."

Hegel, the German philosopher: "Only one man ever understood me." Pause. "And he didn't understand me."

Henry Thoreau, when asked if he had made his peace with God: "I was not aware that we had quarreled."

As professor of vocal physiology at Boston University, Alexander Graham Bell [the inventor of the telephone] had many deaf pupils, including Mabel Hubbard, who later became his wife. . . . As he lay dying, Mabel whispered to him, "Don't leave me." Unable to speak, Bell traced with his fingers the sign "no." With that last silent message, [he] took his final leave.

CLIFTON FADIMAN, *The Little Brown Book of Anecdotes*

An elderly Georgia lady, famed for her Southern hospitality: "Come on, everybody, the food is on the table."

Captain Robert Scott's expedition reached the South Pole in November 1912 and started back, only to be assaulted by blizzards of unprecedented ferocity. Exhaustion and starvation gave them no choice but to make camp. One officer, Lieutenant L. E. G. Oates, was suffering from frostbitten feet, and gangrene had set in, crippling him. He begged the others to press on, leaving him behind, but they refused. Oates struggled up. "I am just going outside," he said, "and may be some time." He stepped out into the storm and was never seen again.

(His heroic sacrifice was in vain; Scott and the rest of his party died before reaching their base camp.)

God will pardon me; it's his job.

HEINRICH HEINE

In *Hodgepodge*, I reported that—in response to his family's assurance that he would soon be well enough to revisit his beloved Bognor—King George V's last words were "Bugger Bognor!" But a disrespectful legend has it that his actual last words were the noble inquiry, "How stands the Empire?" to which a flippant courtier answered, "Fine, Your Majesty! And the Palladium and the Criterion too."

Julius Caesar: *"Et tu, Brute?"* But Sir Oswald Mosley says in *My Life*, "Caesar is credibly reported to have said, *'Kai su teknon,'* rather than *'Et tu, Brute.'* The habit of such Romans was to talk Greek with intimates, in rather the same way as French was used in the court of Frederick the Great."

O. Henry's last words are popularly believed to have been, "Turn up the light! I don't want to go home in the dark." But he may also have said, "For God's sake, won't somebody give me another drink of liquor?"

Edgar Allan Poe: "God help my poor soul!"

Laughter

No one either laughs or smiles in the Bible. Pliny writes in his *Natural History*, "Cassius . . . was never known to laugh all his lifetime, and thereupon was called 'Agelastus,' " unsmiling. (Pliny also lists two other persons whose reticences he seems to find eccentric: Drusus' wife, "who was never known to spit," and Pomponius, "who never belched.")

Neither do animals laugh, of course, "laughing hyenas" to the contrary. And I remember an Australian bird called "the laughing jackass"—the kookaburra. There was a trained nurse in a military hospital out there, a Miss Burroughs, who had a peculiarly exacerbating bedside manner and a laugh to match. Inevitably, we patients knew poor Miss Burroughs as "the Kook."

Wit must amuse; it may make us smile, but it seldom provokes loud laughter, which is the province of humor.

F. SEYMOUR SMITH

Laughter is the shortest distance between two persons.

VICTOR BORGE

Man is the only animal that laughs and weeps; for he is the only animal that is struck with the difference between what things are, and what they ought to be.

WILLIAM HAZLITT, *On Wit and Humor*

A witty thing never excites laughter; it pleases only the mind and never distorts the countenance.

LORD CHESTERFIELD

Laughter, like a silver chain tinkling on a wine glass.

NORMAN WINTHROPE

The loud laugh that spoke the vacant mind.

OLIVER GOLDSMITH, *The Deserted Village*

She laughs at everything you say. Why? Because she has fine teeth.

BENJAMIN FRANKLIN

144

... that older and greater church to which I belong: the church where the oftener you laugh the better because by laughter only can you destroy evil without malice, and affirm good fellowship without mawkishness.

GEORGE BERNARD SHAW

"Laws"

THE MOST FAMOUS of these "Laws" is Murphy's, which says, "If anything can go wrong, it will." Two additional laws have been ascribed to Murphy: "Nothing is as easy as it looks," and "Everything will take longer than you had expected."

Parkinson's Law: "Work expands to fill the time available for its completion."

Steinbeck's Laws (a selection): "3 A, When brandy beckons, no seconds. 3B, When the martini calls, balls! 4, Never let a drunk catch your eye. 5, If you wonder whether you are U, you aren't." ("U" refers to Nancy Mitford's tests for Upper-class and non-Upper-class persons.)

Bryan's Law: "When you decide that you have waited long enough for an answer to your letter and write to request it, your second letter will cross the answer in the mail."

146

Bryan's wife's Law: "If the door/window is open, close it; if it is closed, open it."

Bryan's dog's Law: "If I'm in, I want out; if I'm out, I want in."

Farr's Law for biographers: "The more eminent the man, the more insufferable his widow." And his Law for dealing with two abrasive associates of his: "If you want to like X, go and talk with Y. If you want to like Y, go and talk with X."

Burnham's Laws (a selection): "3. Just as good isn't. 10. If there is no alternative, there is no problem."

Alva Johnston's Law for reporters: "Always carry two pencils." And his Law for aspiring writers: "Nobody ever remembers the name of the man who wrote the article. The short story, yes, and sometimes the poem. But never the author of an article."

Robin Held's Law: "If something is stuck and won't run, slam it against the wall. That'll fix it every time."

Stanley Walker's Law: "Associate with people of cultivated tastes, and some of the culture may rub off on you. Hang around musical folk and you may, with luck, get to know Brahms from Beethoven. But keep company with the very rich and you'll end picking up the check." (Stanley was city editor of the *New York Herald-Tribune*.)

Condensed from LUCIUS BEEBE, *The Big Spenders*

Bryan's Law No. 2: "If six people come to your house for drinks, they will ask for at least four different kinds."

Bryan's Law No. 3: "If you have only one day for business in a foreign city, that day will turn out to be a holiday."

Rosemary Dyer's Law: "Whenever there's something you want to do, you have to do something else first."

If it ain't broke, don't fix it.

Lawyers and the Law

BIOLOGICAL LABORATORIES have stopped using rats for their experiments—they now use lawyers. The scientists don't become attached to them; furthermore, there are some things even a rat won't do.

Anon.

The law is a sort of hocus-pocus science that smiles in your face while it picks your pocket.

CHARLES MACKLIN

If you have ten thousand regulations, you destroy all respect for the law.

SIR WINSTON CHURCHILL

If law school is so hard to get through, how come there are so many lawyers?

CALVIN TRILLIN

149

Lawyers are the only persons in whom ignorance of the law is not punished.

JEREMY BENTHAM

The law, in its majestic equality, forbids the rich as well as the poor to sleep under bridges, to beg in the streets, and to steal bread.

ANATOLE FRANCE

For certain people, after fifty, litigation takes the place of sex.

GORE VIDAL

If one person falsely claims to be married to another, he/she is guilty of jactitation of marriage.

The first thing we do, let's kill all the lawyers.

SHAKESPEARE, *Henry VI, Part II*

Longevity

EVERY DAY IN AMERICA, forty Americans turn 100; about 5,800 become 65, and 8,000 try to forget their fortieth birthdays.

TOM PARKER, *In One Day*

Moses lived	120 years
Abraham	175
Adam	930
Noah	950

A mermaid may live 300 years, according to "The Little Mermaid," by Hans Christian Andersen.

The Pharaoh Pepi II ascended the throne at six and reigned ninety-one years.

I am long on ideas, but short on time. I expect to live to be only about a hundred.

THOMAS A. EDISON, *Golden Book*

The best he could do was eighty-four.

Born in Liberia, Charlie Smith was kidnapped and sold as a slave in New Orleans when he was twelve. According to the Social Security Administration, he was 133 in 1976 and was the oldest person in the United States.

BERNIE SMITH, *The Joy of Trivia*

The actor Charles Macklin played Shylock when he was 100 years old. Born in 1690, he died in 1797. If he could have survived until 1801, he would have lived in three centuries.

Princess Stolberg, the mother-in-law of Charles Edward Stuart, the Young Pretender (1721–88), outlived him by thirty-eight years.

In 1815, the Duc de Richelieu's widow was heard to remark, "As Louis XIV once said to my husband—" In 1815, Louis XIV had been dead for exactly one hundred years.

A correspondent wrote to the *Times* of London in 1910, "My grandfather was twelve years old when Charles I was executed." (1649).

"The First Cuckoo," *The Times* of London

Benjamin Franklin (1706–90) was the grandson of a man who had been born in the sixteenth century, during the reign of Queen Elizabeth I—three generations thus extending to nearly three centuries.

C. CHAMBERS, The Book of Days

Perhaps the most famous of these centenarians was Thomas Parr, of Shropshire, who was born in 1483 and lived to be 152. He married for the first time at 80, and for the second at 126. Rubens painted him; John Taylor, the Water Poet, wrote a poem to him, and when he finally died (1635), he was buried in Westminster Abbey. The highest honor did not come to him until this century, when a distiller named a brand of Scotch whiskey "Old Parr."

Memory
(CONT'D)

DAZZLING AS ARE THE FEATS of memory related in the first *Hodgepodge*, they seem pale and feeble when compared with those of a Russian whom we know only as "S" and only through a book called *The Mind of a Mnemonist*, by Professor A. R. Luria.

I don't think I need cite more than two of S's performances. First, he was shown a list (here abbreviated) of nonsense monosyllables:

1. ma va na sa na va
2. na sa na ma va
3. sa na ma va na
4. va sa na va na ma
5. na va na va sa ma
6. na ma sa ma va na
7. sa ma sa va na
8. na sa ma va ma na

Asked to repeat it, he did so without hesitation or error and was able to repeat it again *four years later*!

Second, he was shown this utterly meaningless "mathematical formula":

$$N \cdot \sqrt{d^2 \times \frac{85}{vx}} \cdot \sqrt{\frac{276^2 \cdot 86x}{n^2v \cdot \pi264}} \, n^2b = sv \frac{1624}{32^2} \cdot r^2s$$

According to Professor Luria, S shut his eyes, paused as he "looked the material over" in his mind, and in seven minutes came through with an exact reproduction.

After such demonstrations, I hesitate to mention S's less spectacular tricks, but here are two of them: He could speed or slow his pulse at will, and he could raise or lower the temperature of his right and left hand independently. Professor Luria asks, "How was it *possible?*" He gives no answer, and, Lord knows, I can't help him!

An adult can memorize a list of 36 nonsense syllables in 22 seconds.

STUART A. SANDOW, *Durations*

At a meeting at George Washington University in 1988, Hans Eberstar demonstrated that he had memorized *pi* to 11,944 places.

Sir Winston Churchill is said to have memorized all twelve books of *Paradise Lost* in one week.

Mighty Men

TWO MIGHTY MEN who come to mind at once are Samson and Goliath. The Bible cites none of Goliath's feats, but it says of Samson that he "rent" a young lion, slew a thousand men with the jawbone of an ass, and pulled down the pillars of a house— among numerous other feats. And there are plenty of other mighty men whose performances are well authenticated:

John Ericsson, the Swede who designed the *Monitor* . . . asked two workmen in his shop to move a bar of iron he had tripped on. They said it was too heavy. He looked at them, picked it up, carried it, and threw it on the scrap pile. They put it on a scale later and found that it weighed six hundred pounds.

CARL SANDBURG, *Abraham Lincoln, the War Years*

Few were aware of the physical strength of Mr. Lincoln. In muscular power he was one in a thousand. One morning, sitting on deck [of a revenue cutter], he saw an ax in a socket on the bulwarks, and taking it up, held it at arm's length at the extremity of the helve with this thumb and forefinger, continuing to hold it there for a number of minutes. The most powerful sailors on board tried in vain to imitate him. Mr. Lincoln said he could do this when he was eighteen ... and had never seen a day since that time when he could not.

IB.

Joe Stecher, the professional wrestler, could mount a horse and squeeze it between his knees until it lay down.

Jackson, a heavyweight boxing champion of early nineteenth-century England, could tie a thirteen-pound weight to his little finger and hold it at arm's length.

King Pedro Pereira of Portugal (seventeenth century) broke iron horseshoes with his hands. Somebody in mythology could core an apple with his forefinger and somebody else could fell an ox with a blow of his fist. I remember reading about them, but I've forgotten their names. Sorry! Nor do I know what feats of strength were performed by Angus MacAskill of Scotland (1825–63), but he was billed as "the strongest man on record," and it is authentic that his chest was sixty-five inches around and his weight was 525 pounds.

> Under a spreading chestnut-tree
>   The village smithy stands;
> The smith, a mighty man is he,
>   With large and sinewy hands;
> And the muscles of his brawny arms
>   are strong as iron bands.

HENRY WADSWORTH LONGFELLOW, "The Village Blacksmith"

The Fourth Form felt it obligatory to recite these last two lines as,

> The muscles of his scrawny arms
>   Are strong as rubber bands.

According to William Hutton, writing of a visit to Derby, England, in 1857, "Thomas Topham, thirty years old, standing five feet ten, performed the following feats, rolling up a pewter dish as a man rolls up a sheet of paper; holding a pewter quart at arm's length and squeezing the sides together; lifting two hundredweight with his little finger and moving it gently over his head. He lifted an oak table six feet long with his teeth, although half a hundredweight was hung to the extremity. He took Mr. Chambers, vicar of All Saints, who weighed twenty-seven stone [378 pounds], and raised him with one hand. His head being laid on one chair and his feet on another, four people, fourteen stone each [196 pounds], sat upon his body, which he heaved at pleasure. He struck a round bar of iron, one inch diameter, against his naked arm, and at one stroke bent it like a bow. Weakness and feeling seemed fled altogether. . . ."

In the mid-1920s, a retired German U-boat captain, Count Felix von Luckner, toured American colleges and universities demonstrating the prodigious strength of his hands and arms. His shows were popular; everybody liked him, partly because he had sunk fifteen (I think) Allied cargo ships without the loss of a single life. I remember that he had a forearm the size of Popeye's. One of his feats was to stand a billiard cue upright on its butt, take its tip between his forefinger and middle finger, palm up, then reverse his hand, rolling his forefinger over the middle until the cue was butt-up. Try it with an umbrella!

Another feat was to seat a man in a kitchen chair, grasp a front leg of the chair with one hand, and pick up chair, man, and all. Still another—and this, he told us, required not only great strength, but real delicacy—was to lace his fingers around a small coffee cup and squeeze it slowly, slowly, until it was egg-shaped.

He said he had built up the strength of his hands by squeezing a tennis ball when he was off duty. I wouldn't be surprised if he could have crushed a polo ball into toothpicks.

Superman and Spider Man: no comment.

Miscellaneous
(CONT'D)

NOTE FOR CHEFS: eight pinches equal a teaspoonful; six drops equal a dash.

Mustapha Kemal Ataturk, who founded the modern Turkish republic, died at 9:05 A.M. on November 10, 1938, in Dolma Bagche Palace, Istanbul. All the palace clocks were stopped at that moment, and have never been restarted.

Autobiography is an unrivaled vehicle for telling the truth about other people.

PHILIP GUEDALLA

The leading cargo shipped out of Tampa International Airport is tropical fish; the second leader is human remains.

One friend in a lifetime is much; two are many; three are barely possible. Friendship needs a certain parallelism of life, a community of thought, a rivalry of aim.

HENRY JAMES

161

Television enables you to be entertained in your home by people you wouldn't have in your home.

DAVID FROST

Good judgment comes from experience, and experience comes from bad judgment.

BARRY LAPATNER

A liberal is someone whose interests aren't at stake at the moment.

WILLIS PLAYER

Very ugly or very beautiful women should be flattered on their understanding, mediocre ones, on their beauty.

LORD CHESTERFIELD

I should have praised you more had you praised me less.

LOUIS XIV

Traffic congestion in large cities should be blamed on the greed of the property developers and the short-sightedness of city planners. Few people realize that it takes eighty-seven truckloads daily to service a single high-rise building.

NORMAN HICKMAN

It is better to be beautiful than to be good. But it is better to be good than to be ugly.

OSCAR WILDE

In Britain's Foreign Office, no one may use red ink except an ambassador, who uses it to make marginal notes on documents.

Martyrdom is the only way in which a man can become famous without ability.

GEORGE BERNARD SHAW

The most happy marriage I can picture ... would be the union of a deaf man to a blind woman.

SAMUEL TAYLOR COLERIDGE

The clocks at the Greenwich Observatory, England, were stopped for one second at midnight on December 31, 1979, to give the year an extra second, which it needed because of the slightly slower rotation of the earth.

A different taste in jokes is a great strain on the affections.

GEORGE ELIOT

Margaret Countess of Birkenhead made funny stories about her unforgettable husband even funnier. She was a fine amateur singer and went one day to the Waterford Asylum in Oxford to entertain the mental patients. "When in full flight," she narrated, "I suddenly noticed that the whole of the front row had their fingers firmly stuck in their ears. And when I sat down at the end of the song, there was my husband beside me, not consoling me for my humiliation, but saying in an audible whisper, 'You see, they're not so mad after all.'"

ELIZABETH LONGFORD, *The Pebbled Shore*

St. John Street, in Rome, is only nineteen inches wide; and One Person Street, in Brussels, is so-called because it is too narrow for two to walk abreast.

Things I had to learn the hard way:

1. Don't walk on a slippery surface with your hands in your pockets.

2. Fill in the stub and *then* write your check.

3. When you want to unscrew the tin cap of a bottle, grasp the cap firmly in one hand, and turn the bottle with the other. This way, you run no risk of cutting your fingers.

A REGARDS ring is one set with jewels whose initials form the word REGARDS: ruby—emerald—garnet—amethyst—ruby—diamond—sapphire.

The motto "In God We Trust" didn't appear on U.S. currency until 1864.

G. K. Chesterton wrote a poem with the title:
"PLAKKOPYTRIXPHYLISPERADAULANTIOBATRIX"

When asked which of the Gabors was the eldest, Zsa-Zsa said, "She'll never admit it, but it's Mama."

A toast: "May you never meet a mouse in your cupboard with tears in his eyes!"

J. C. FURNAS

Charlie Chaplin's genius was in comedy. He had no sense of humor.

LITA CHAPLIN, his ex-wife

Good breeding consists in concealing how much we think of ourselves and how little we think of others.

ORSON WELLES

Sam Goldwyn may never have said "A verbal contract isn't worth the paper it's written on," or any of the other malapropisms attributed to him, but there's no doubt that the following are authentic:

President Coolidge: "When more and more people are out of work, unemployment results."

President Eisenhower: "Things have never been more like they are today in history."

President Lyndon Johnson: "For the first time in history, profits are higher than ever before."

Yogi Berra: "Nobody goes to that restaurant any more. It's too crowded."

Bunny McLeod: "It was so dark, you couldn't see your face in front of you."

Celebrated shapes:
Trafalgar Square, Dupont Circle, the Oval Office, the Round Table, the Pentagon, Marilyn Monroe.

Nothing makes a man feel so inadequate as his inability to get a taxi for his wife on a rainy night.

The Peruvian Navy commissioned its first submarine in 1879 —twenty-one years before the U.S. commissioned its own first.

The plot of many of Horatio Alger's inspirational novels for juveniles centers on a poor but honest boy who makes a fortune through pluck and luck. Alger himself died a pauper.

Names
(CONT'D)

Of Animals

THE DALLAS ZOO has two yaks, "Yack" and "Yill."

The John Steinbecks' poodle turned around so many times before lying down that they nicknamed him the "Whirlpoodle." And I've been told of a collie whose name, "Fido," is spelled "Phideaux."

My peacock likes to roost on the edge of the roof, so we call him "the Gutter-Percher."

Of all pet names, I like best the one a friend of mine gave her canary: "Ten-Zing," because he is a faithful chirper.

Of French Hotels

Bob Littell, late a roving editor of *Reader's Digest*, made a hobby of collecting the bizarre names of French hotels: the St.

James and d'Alvny, in Paris; the Montgomery and the West; the Immaculate Conception and the Post at Lourdes; and a dozen others. Whenever he or I spotted a candidate for his list, we would jeer at the foolish French. And then—and then we suddenly realized that many American newspapers have names that are a compound of elements even more absurdly disparate. What American, with a copy of his hometown Lamar, Colorado, *Daily News and Holly Chieftain* sticking from his coat pocket, is truly entitled to laugh at Saint-Michel's Hotel of the Epicure and the Holy Spirit? How about the Watsonville, California, *Register-Pajaronian Sun?* The Centerville, Iowa, *Ad Express and Daily Iowegian?* And over in Missouri, the *Moberly Monitor-Index & Democrat?* . . . Spain is another matter. It stands alone and unchallenged with its Hotel Sexy.

What has become of the old-fashioned given names that were so popular in America a century and more ago—Silas, Ezra, Caleb, Hiram, Joshua? You rarely hear them now.

Apropos given names with a religious flavor, "St. George" has been a favorite in our family for generations. In recent years, a great-uncle, my father, a son, a grandson, and several cousins have all been St. Georges. When the Pope desanctified the original St. George a few years ago, my brother and I lost no time in trimming our kinsmen down to a simple "George." Very satisfying. As for family names, by far the oddest I ever encountered is Strong i' th' arm. If you doubt me, look in the London telephone directory and you'll find "Strong i' th' arm, Jewelers & Silversmiths, 13 Dover St. W 1."

Of Residences

Alec Woollcott called his apartment Wits' End, and Dorothy Parker called hers Rising Gorge.

Bill Ballard and I once spent a month in a suburb of Istanbul called Rumeli Hisar ("European Castle"). Our pension had the forbidding name of "Yilanli Yali," which means "the House of Snakes on the Waterfront." There was no doubt about the waterfront; we could flick cigarette butts from our balcony into the Bosphorus. But snakes? Our landlord told us that in the bad old days of the Sultanate, the house had caught the eye of a rich and powerful pasha, who notified the then owner that he wished to buy it, and would call that afternoon to close the deal. There was no nonsense about "Will you sell?" The pasha wished to buy, so the owner damn-well *had* to sell. But wait. When the pasha presented himself, and they had drunk the ceremonial cups of thick coffee, the owner dug deep into his imagination and came up with this: "I must warn Your Highness that my poor house is infested with snakes. Big, ugly, poisonous ones, as big as Your Highness' forearm. We have tried everything to rid ourselves of them, but nothing avails." Of course, no snake had ever been seen in the house, or near it. But at that moment a yellow and brown snake with a stubby tail started crawling across the tile floor. The pasha bolted in terror, and the owner lived there happily ever afterward. So did Ballard and I, though only for a month.

Ed Applewhite wants to buy a sheltered waterfront property, just so he can call it Grudge Harbor. (I've heard of a riverside house called Mouthwater, but I can't vouch for it.) Surely, somewhere in the South, there's a manor called Yew Hall? If there isn't, there ought to be.

I thought I had suffered every possible inconvenience, frustration, and embarrassment that could come from having a "III" attached to one's name. Strangers begin their letters, "Dear Mr. III." A Hollywood gossip columnist referred to me as J.B. Three-Eyes. I have also been King Joseph III. And so—painfully—on. But a friend of mine with a name like my own —I'll call him Richard Roe III—recently had an experience in London, where he registered at a hotel and told the clerk that he was expecting a number of rather important telephone calls, so please notify the operator at once of his arrival. The afternoon passed, and the evening, and the next day, and not one of his calls came through, not even the call from Washington that his wife had promised to make. Puzzled, he called *her* and received an ice-cold greeting—no "How are you" or "How was the trip?" or "Is everything all right?" but a chill "Where are you?"

168

"In my room at the hotel. Why?"

"Because I've called you three times in the past twenty-four hours, and each time the operator has said you didn't answer. Where have you been? What have you been doing?"

"I've been here all the time." And the sad dialogue of suspicion, accusation, protestation, and bewilderment went on until the infuriated Roe broke it off by rushing to the lobby and demanding to see the manager. This, incredibly, is what had happened:

His sprawling signature had overflowed the line reserved for it on the registration card, and the "III" had gone into the next line—the one for the number of his room. All calls for him had thus gone to Room 111.

Of Streets

One of my pleasures in travel is collecting strange and wonderful street names in foreign cities. For instance, Man in the Moon Passage, in London; Boy, Wait for Me Alley, in Lisbon; Meat and Bread Street, Brussels; the Street of the Lovely Leaves, Paris; Adam's Rib Street, Luxembourg; and dozens, scores of others no less delightful.

And then I come home to 19th and J, Washington, D.C.; 12th and Walnut, Philadelphia; 39th and Park, New York—flat, dull insipid. I don't say that America draws all its street names from the same stale stock—Broad, Main, State, First, Second, Oak, Elm, Railroad, Capitol, Market and their dreary like—but there must be a happy medium between these platitudes and the "realtors'" pretentious elegancies, such as Crestview, Burnholme, and Woodmere. I am thinking of Catfish Row, Charleston; Skunk's Misery Lane, Locust Valley, Long Island; Monkey Wrench Lane, Bristol, Rhode Island; and Three Chopt Road, here in Richmond.

I have strong feelings on this subject and I could pursue it further, but then I think of what happened to the late author and gourmet, Julian Street. *Collier's* commissioned him to do a series of travel articles about American communities. One of them was Cripple Creek, Colorado, where he happened to stroll down Myers Avenue, and fall into conversation with a raucous

169

red-headed woman who informed him that he was in the heart of the red-light district, and that her name was Madame Leo. She was an interesting and amusing old broad, and Street reported the interview at some length. When *Collier's* published it, Cripple Creek was outraged and took instant revenge. The city fathers changed the name of Myers Avenue to "Julian Street."

Rudy Vallee tried to persuade the town officials of Hollywood Hills, California, to change the name of the street where he lived to Rue de Vallee. No dice.

Instead of counting sheep on a "white night," try listing streets celebrated in popular songs. Here are a few:

Piccadilly ("Tipperary"), Fifth Avenue ("Easter Parade"), State Street ("Chicago"), Second Avenue ("Second-hand Rose"), Beale Street and Basin Street ("Blues"), Old Kent Road, Broadway ("Give my Regards to . . ."), the Bowery ("We never go there any more"), Basin Street ("Where all the light folks and the dark folks meet"), Forty-second Street, the Strand ("I'm Burlington Bertie, I rise at ten-thirty and go for a stroll down the Strand").

For the Telephone

Half the time I have to give my name over the telephone, it comes back "Brown" or "Bryant" or "O'Brien."

"No," I say, heating up. "Bryan—Bry-yan."

Then, as if I'd said "Brzienciwc," I get "Spell it, please."

To keep my irritation from boiling over, I remind myself of friends whose names are far more difficult to establish than my own. For instances, some cousins of mine whose name is pronounced "Tolliver," but spelled "Taliaferro." And the Tayloes, with an "e." And Admiral Bill Schoech, pronounced "Shay" (or when he is out of range "Shucks" and "Shoosh"). Kinloch is pronounced "Kin-law." Nalle is "Nawl." Michaux is "Misher." And I think of all those French Huguenot names in South Carolina: Huger (You-*jee*), Prioleau (*Pray*-lo) Horry (O-*ree*), and the rest.

170

The late General Latané Montague, U.S.M.C., liked to tell about his first day as a private in the Corps. When the roll was called, no one answered to the name "Mon-taig," so young Montague ventured to tell the sergeant that his name was actually "Mont-a-gue." The sergeant studied him for a full minute before announcing, "Very well, Mont-a-gue. Four hours' fat-i-gue."

And Titles, Correct and Official

The Chief Justice of the Supreme Court is correctly Chief Justice of the United States.

The British monarch is Queen Elizabeth the Second.

The Cunard liner is correctly RMS *Queen Elizabeth Two*. She was named not for the present monarch, or for her mother, also Queen Elizabeth, but for a previous RMS *Queen Elizabeth*.

The *Monitor* didn't fight the *Merrimack*, but the *Virginia*, rechristened when Confederates took over the U.S.S. *Merrimack*.

The early and still official name of Rhode Island is The Rhode Island and Providence Plantations.

The official name of the Smithsonian Museum is the United States National Museum.

The official name of Westminster Abbey is the Collegiate Church of St. Peter in Westminster, and the official name of the Tower of London is the Royal Palace and Fortress of the Tower of London.

The real name of the company that controls most of Monte Carlo is the Socíeté des Bains de Mer et du Cercle des Étrangers.

Persons' Real Names

Mata Hari's real name was Gertrude Margarete MacLeod (née Zelle).

Harry Houdini's real name was Erich Weiss.

The real name of Pélé, the great soccer player, is M. H. Edson Arantes do Nascimento.

Scaasi, the fashionable New York couturier, is "Isaacs" spelled backward.

Casey Jones's real name was John Luther Jones. His nickname had nothing to do with Kansas City; it came from his having been born near Cayce, Kentucky.

The real name of Nadar, the great pioneer French photographer, was Félix Tournachon.

The real name of the explorer and journalist, Henry M. Stanley (1841–1904), was John Rowlands or Rollantt.

Grover Cleveland was christened "Stephen Grover Cleveland," Woodrow Wilson was christened "Thomas Woodrow Wilson," and Calvin Coolidge was christened "John Calvin Coolidge."

Persons and Places

The English take pride in far-out names. I've met "Sir A. fforde" in the newspapers, and the "ffollikott" family, and you can find Admiral Sir Reginald Aylmer Ranfurly Plunkett-Ernle-Erles-Drax in *Who's Who*. But if English family names strike you as bizarre, try some of their pronunciations.

Ruthven	*pronounced*	Rivven
Menzies		Mingies
Cholmondeley		Chumley
Beauchamp		Beecham
Marjoribanks		Marchbanks
Belvoir		Beever

I'm not going to get into the spelling and pronunciation of English place names, or we'll be here all day. I can cite dozens of oddities, but a single one will serve the purpose. "Cirencester," pronounced "*Siss*-is-ter."

Nature Notes
(CONT'D)

ALL THE FOLLOWING BELONG to one class of what?

Pink Kisser	Kuhliloach
Tiger Barb	Corydoras Cat
Head and Tail Lite	Marble Angel
Serpa Tetra	Plecostomus
Velvet Sword	Rummy Nose
Salt and Pepper Platy	

Answer: Tropical fish for the aquarium.

The average one-acre grassy field may harbor 1.25 million spiders.

MARK TRAIL

The fibers of five Merino [sheep], joined end to end, could tie a bow around the world.

NINA HYDE, "Fabric of History: Wool," *National Geographic*, May 1988

[God] seems to have an inordinate fondness for beetles.

J. B. S. HALDANE

Old Faithful, the most famous geyser in Yellowstone National Park, is far from being as punctual as tradition asserts and its name implies. Instead of erupting every 60 minutes some 24 times a day, it actually may erupt between 18 and 21 times a day and at intervals between 34 and 106 minutes. A Park authority says that the interval has been lengthening over the past twenty-five years "because of earthquake activity and human vandalism."

Jamaicans used to club fruit trees that remained barren.

The narwhal's tusk may be half as long as its body.

Just as human beings are right- or left-handed, elephants are right- or left-tusked.

The fastest growing member of the plant world is the bamboo, a grass, which has been known to grow a full 16 inches in 24 hours, and to attain a height of 120 feet.

I know nothing about the potto beyond that it is a West African lemur. I don't need to know even that little. Its mere name suffices me. I can play with it for hours: "Giotto's motto was, 'You ought to not meet a blotto potto in a grotto.'" Take it from there!

The Japanese have bred a duck that can't quack.

If a rabbit's incisors were not abraded by gnawing, they would grow 20 inches a year, and achieve a total length of some 10 feet in the animal's lifetime.

There is a persistent belief among people who should know better that the red fox is a feline and the gray fox a canine. This is absurd; both are vulpines. According to the TV program *Nature*, the red fox is "the most widely spread and successful of all carnivores." More so than the rat? Or isn't the rat carnivorous?

Dogs sweat through their tongues, cattle through their noses.

A flea can jump 12 inches, the equivalent of a man's jumping the length of six city blocks.

Jack rabbits are so named because their long ears are like a jackass's.

The shark was named after the card shark, not the other way round.

J. R. C.

A shrew's heart beats close to 1,000 times a minute.

What follows is a phonetic transcription of a nightingale's song, made by a French composer. I have borrowed it from an extract made by *The New York Times* from a book, *Michelangelo's Snowman: A Commonplace Collection*, by George Herrick.

Tiou, tiou, tiou, tiou—Spe, tiou, squa—tio, tio, tio, tio, tio, tio, tio, tío, tíx—Coutio, coutio, coutio, coutio—Squo, squo, squo, squo—Tzu, tzu, tzu, tzu, tzu, tzu, tzu, tzu, tzi

—Corror, tiou, squa, pipiqui—Zozozozozozozozozozo-zozo, zirrhading—Tsissisi, tsissisisisisisisis—Dzoree, dzo-ree, dzoree, tzatu, dzi—Dlo, dlo, dlo, dlo, dlo, dlo, dlo, dlo, dlo—Quio, trrrrrrrrr—Lu, lu, lu, lu, ly, ly, ly, ly, lie, lie, lie, lie—Quio didl li lulylie—Hagurr, gurr, quipio—Coui, coui, coui, couri, qui, qui, qui, gai, gui, gui, gui—Goll, goll, goll, goll guia hadadoi—Conigui, horr, ha diadia dill si—Hezezezezezezezezezezezezezezeze couar ho dze hoi—Quia, quia, quia, quia, quia, quia, quia, quia, ti Ki, ki, ki, io, io, io, ioioioio ki—Lu ly li le lai la leu lo, didl io, quia—Kigaigaigaigaigaigaigai guiagaigaigai couior dzio dzio pi.

Some 10 trillion mosquitoes—that's 10 million million—buzz about the United States every year, which is about 41,000 per inflamed and itching capita of our citizens. Only the females bite, each of them one to four times in her life. There's no escaping them. They come in 2,500 varieties and range from northern Alaska to southern Brazil, and they can survive temperatures from 100 degrees to below freezing.

GEORGE STABLEY JR.,
Condensed from *Ducks Unlimited*

Spider-web silk is stronger for its size than any other fiber in nature. It is also so elastic that it can stretch one-fifth its length without breaking. Though the thread looks delicate, it has a tensile strength greater than that of steel.

HY GARDNER

The prolific possum has the shortest known period of gestation in the animal kingdom—13 days. The possum is also the only animal with a forked penis.

Insects have evolved into an estimated 30 million different species, of which one million have been discovered. Insects account for roughly 85 percent of all animal life, and it has been calculated that the combined weight of Earth's insects is 12 times greater than that of its human population.

THOMAS A. BASS, "Africa's Drive to Win the Battle Against Insects," *Smithsonian*, August 1988

The male giant wood [silk] spider (*Nephila maculata*) is only 1/300 the weight and one-tenth the size of the female. She could easily make a meal of him, so he first calms her by binding her with silk. After the mating, he ensures sole paternity by sealing her sex opening with a waxy plug.

Zoogoer, Bulletin of Friends of the National Zoo

Rats caused the Bombay plague epidemic of 1898, which killed 12.5 million Indians. During the Black Plague of the Middle Ages, the rat, as host for the plague-carrying flea, caused an estimated 25 million deaths. In a world haunted by threat of famine, rats will destroy approximately one fifth of all food crops planted. In India their depredations will deprive a hungry people of enough grain to fill a freight train stretching more than 3,000 miles.

THOMAS Y. CANBY, *National Geographic*

The average rat can—
—wriggle through a hole no larger than the diameter of a quarter.
—scale a brick wall as though it had rungs.
—swim half a mile and tread water for three days.
—gnaw through lead pipes and cinder blocks with chisel teeth that exert an incredible 24,000 pounds per square inch.
—survive being flushed down a toilet, and enter buildings by the same route.
—multiply so rapidly that a pair could have 15,000 descendants in a year's life span.
—plummet five stories to the ground and scurry off unharmed.

IB.

When former *Smithsonian* magazine editor Edwards Park was a member of the *National Geographic*'s staff, he learned he was being sent on assignment to Machu Picchu and sought illustrations editor Kip Ross's advice. "Watch out for snakes," Ross warned him.

Ted Park, hating snakes, pressed Ross for details and learned that Ross, while riding mule back up to the high ridge upon which the Lost City of the Incas had been built, had heard little

177

rustling noises in the grass along the trail and asked his guide, "Pedro, what is that?"

"Señor," the guide said, "that is a fer-de-lance."

"Oh my God!" Ross said. The fer-de-lance, he knew, was a species of large, extremely dangerous pit viper that infests those parts. Ross and the guide rode together in silence for a few minutes then Ross asked, "Pedro, what happens if I get bitten by a fer-de-lance? What do I do?"

Pedro thought for a moment and answered, "Señor, you *compose* yourself."

C. D. B. BRYAN, *The National Geographic Society: One Hundred Years of Adventure & Discovery*

Nostalgia

Some Slang from Yesterday and the Day Before

GIRLS WERE CHICKENS, frails, babes, bimbos (or simply bims, as in "a plenty nutsy bim"), dishes, tomatoes, cookies, tootsies, dames.

Money was scratch, the ready, spondulix, the long green, mazuma.

A drunk was sozzled, stinko, gassed, pie-eyed, boiled, fried, tight (as Dick's hatband), cock-eyed, plastered.

And when the cake eaters, snakes, and drugstore cowboys weren't mashing or spooning or necking or pitching woo, they were saying things like this:

Hold yer hosses! . . . Here's your hat, what's your hurry? . . . Officer, call a cop! . . . Operance, operance, I want an ambulator! . . . Ixnay! . . . Ninny on your tintype . . . Isch ka bibble . . . I should worry . . . You tell 'em, corset, you've been around the women. . . . Paddle your own canoe. . . . My fadder's mustache

179

... So's yer old man ... Buy a drum and beat it ... Horse feathers ... Tell it to the Marines ... That's all she wrote ... You tell 'em goldfish; you've been around the globe ... Twenty-three skiddoo! ... I love my wife, but, oh, you kid! ... Excuse my dust ... Hold 'er, Newt! She's a-headin fer the pea-patch ... Don't spit, remember the Flood ... banana oil ... Jeez, me beads! ... You said a mouthful ... Long time no see ... Get a horse.... Pardon my wet glove.... Oh, you beautiful doll! ... Look, Ma, no hands.... I faw down and go boom.... So long, Abyssinia.... Love me, love my dog.... You tell 'em, brassière; you've been over the bumps.

Old Friends from the Advertisements of Fifty Years Ago

Mr. Coffee Nerves and Mr. Thirsty Fibre ... Peter and Polly Ponds ... Phoebe Snow of the Lackawanna Railroad ("the Road of Anthracite") ... Velvet Joe and Chubbins ... the Fisk Tire boy, yawning ("Time to Re-Tire") ... the Arrow Collar man ... the Old Dutch Cleanser girl ("Chases Dirt") ... Lionel Strongfort and Charles Atlas ... the Campbell Soup kids ... the McCallum Hosiery girl ... the Gold Dust Twins ("Let the Gold Dust Twins Do Your Work") ... the Seven Sutherland Sisters ... Lydia Pinkham ... the White Rock nymph ... Mother Winslow, of the soothing syrup ... the Daisy air-rifle kid.

Old Friends from Old Cartoonia

Flash Gordon, Dr. Zarkov, and Ming the Merciless ... Andy Gump, Min, and Uncle Bim ("Soup's on") ... Happy Hooligan and Maud Mule ("Don't get hoited!") ... George Bungle of Sunken Heights ... Little Nemo and Flip ... the Katzenjammer Kids (Hans und Fritz), der Captain und der Inspector ... Mutt and Jeff, and Jeff's brother Julius, "the strongest little man in the world" ... Barney Google and Sparkplug ... Major and Mrs. Hoople ("Fap!") ... Pogo and Beauregard and Miss Mamzelle ... Harold Teen ... The Terrible-Tempered Mr. Bang, Powerful Katrinka, and Mickey ("Himself") McGuire ... Popeye the Sailor Man ("I yam what I yam"), Olive Oyl, Swee'pea, and

Wimpy ... Percy and Ferdie, the Hallroom Boys ... Jiggs and Maggie, Count Nocount ... Li'l Abner, Moonbeam McSwine, the Schmoos, Big Barnsmell, Hairless Joe, Lonesome Polecat, Daisy Mae, Ma Yokum ... Buck Rogers ... Smilin' Jack ...

Come back! Come back!

Some Primitive Conundrums from my Childhood

When is a door not a door? When it is ajar (a jar—the explanation was always added to make *sure* you understood the joke).

Why need you never starve in the desert? On account of the sand which is (sandwiches) there.

How did Queen Victoria take her medicine? In cider (inside her).

What did the strawberry say to his friend? "If you hadn't been so fresh, we wouldn't be in this jam."

What did the little chicken say when it found an orange in its nest? "Oh, see the orange mama laid."

Why does a chicken cross the road? To get to the other side.

Why does a fireman wear red suspenders? To keep his pants up.

What is the difference between a soldier and an actress? A soldier faces the powder; an actress powders the face.

Numbers

Numbers remind me of images. Take the number 1. This is a proud, well-built man. Number 2 is a high-spirited woman. Number 3 a gloomy person. Number 6, a man with a swollen foot. Number 7 a man with a moustache. Number 8 a very stout woman. As for the number 87, what I see is a fat woman and a man twirling his moustache.

A. R. Luria, The Mind of a Mnemonist

I could never make out what those damned dots meant.

Lord Randolph Churchill, former Chancellor of
the Exchequer, referring to decimal points

Can you think of a piece of fiction in which the characters have numbers, not names? See *Alice in Wonderland*, Chapter 8, "The Queen's Croquet-Ground":

A large rose-tree stood near the entrance of the garden; the roses growing on it were white, but there were three gardeners at it, busily painting them red. . . . Just as [Alice] came up to them, she heard one of them say, "Look out now, Five! Don't go splashing paint over me like that!"

"I couldn't help it," said Five in a sulky tone; "Seven jogged my elbow."

Counting at the rate of one number per second, it would take not quite twelve days to count from 1 to 1 million.

A perfect number equals the sum of its divisors: E.g., 6 equals $1 + 2 + 3$. An abundant number is greater than the sum of its divisors: E.g., 4 is greater than $1 + 2$. A defective (or deficient) number is less than the sum of its divisors: E.g., 12 is less than $1 + 2 + 3 + 4 + 6$.

In the United States and France, 1 trillion is 1 million million. In Great Britain and Germany, it is 1,000 million million. In the United States and France, 1 nonillion is 1 followed by thirty zeros. In Great Britain and Germany, it is 1 followed by fifty-four zeros.

Take a piece of cigarette paper 1/1000th of an inch thick. Tear it in half. Put one half on top of the other and tear it again. Imagine that you can repeat this operation fifty times, doubling the number of pieces of paper each time. How high would the pile be? Answer: 17,769 miles.

JOHN R. COURNYER

The Arabic numerals were originally designed so that each digit contained the number of angles in the value indicated. Thus:

IB.

There is a theory that words we use to represent numbers often go back to the days when people counted on their fingers.

The word "eleven" comes from the Anglo-Saxon word "endleo-fan." Which may have meant "and one left." They counted to ten on their fingers and had "one left"—eleven.

The rows of numbers in this "magic square" add up to 34 in ten different directions, horizontally, diagonally, and vertically.

A megaparsec, a unit of measure for interstellar space, is equal to 19 million million million miles or 3.26 million light-years.

The black friends of my childhood liked to challenge a stranger to count to 100 faster than they could. This is how they did it: "Ten, ten, double-ten, forty-five, fifteen." And here's how our handyman, Unc' Jac Tazewell (pronounced "Taz'l") used to count eggs from the nests into his basket, an egg for each accent:

A ońe, a twó, a threé,
Ah ám a jiḿmy geé.
Ah bét a mán a pínt o' rúm
He cóuld not drínk with mé.
Ah eáts no ḿo', Ah drínks no léss,
An' thár's twén-teé.

And so it is.

In honor of Louis XIV's capture of Luxembourg, some literary trifler composed this chronogram:

DestrVCtIo VrbIs LVXeMboVrgensIs.

Noting that U and V are the same letter in Latin, sift out the letters that are also Roman numerals (here capitalized), arrange them in order (largest to smallest)—MDCLXVVVVIII—and you have the date of the capture: 1683 (actually 1684). Ingenious, eh?

Venerable joke, appended here only because it is apropos:
A Scottish crofter, making his first visit to a city, noticed a handsome building with its cornerstone inscribed "MCMIX." Farther along, he saw another building, even larger, with the same inscription on its cornerstone. "He must've had pots of the stuff, that Mr. McMix," the crofter said.

The famous French mathematician Pierre de Fermat (1605–65) wrote in the margin of a book—opposite a statement that no proof had ever been found for the formula $x^n + y^n = \frac{1}{2}Z^n$—"I have the proof, but it is too long to set down here." Then he died. The proof has never been rediscovered.

In 1963, Donald Gillies, using a computer at the University of Illinois, found that 2 raised to the 11,213th power, minus 1, is a prime.

ANATOLE BECK, MICHAEL N. BLEICHER,
and DONALD W. CROWE,
Excursions into Mathematics

A prime number is divisible only by itself and 1. There are 26 of them—2, 3, 5, 7, 11, and so on—among the first one hundred numbers. But they become steadily rarer, and appear irregularly. After centuries of investigation, no formula for generating all the primes has been found.

IB.

Separated by only one number, 5 and 7 are "twin primes," and so are 101 and 103, and 1,000,000,009,649 and 1,000,000,009,651, but it has never been proved that there is a point beyond which there are no more pairs of primes.

IB.

Arabic numerals didn't begin to enjoy widespread use in Europe until about 1275. Their first recorded appearance on a gravestone was in 1371 and on coins in 1425, in Switzerland.

Among all the numbers, there are only four that are equal to the sum of the cubes of their digits: 153, 370, 371, and 407.

CONSTANCE REID, *From Zero to Infinity*

In 1873 William Shanks calculated the value of *pi* to 707 decimal places, but erred on the 528th place. In 1961, by a strange coincidence, another Shanks, Daniel, with the help of a computer, calculated the value to 100,265 places.

DMITRI BORGMANN, *Language on Vacation*

Old Age

(CONT'D)

Autumn has always been my favorite season, and evening has been for me the pleasantest time of day. I love the sunlight but I cannot fear the coming of the dark.

DUFF COOPER, *Old Men Forget*, last lines

First you are young; then you are middle-aged; then you are old; then you are wonderful.

LADY DIANA COOPER

How old would you be, if you didn't know how old you was?

SATCHEL PAIGE

Old age is not for sissies.

JOSEPH H. MCGINTY AND OTHERS

After a performance, a man called on Sir John Gielgud in his dressing room to congratulate him. "How pleased I am to meet

187

you!" Sir John said. "I used to know your son—we were at school together."

"I have no son," the man replied. "I was at school with you."

CECIL BEATON, *Books of Bricks*,
edited by Robert Morley

By the year 2000, there may be 100,000 persons in the U.S. older than 100.

DR. ROBERT N. BUTLER,
chief of geriatrics,
Mount Sinai Hospital, NYC

You can't help growing older, but you can help growing old.

GEORGE BURNS

I want to die young at a ripe old age.

ASHLEY MONTAGU, anthropologist

Growing old is not a gradual decline, but a series of jumps down from one ledge to another.

KENNETH CLARK,
Another Part of the Wood

I consider the Golden Age as YUK.

LOIS BLAIR JANSEN,
quoted in Malcolm Cowley,
The View from 80

No man attains perfect peace of mind until he has lost his last tooth and all desire for a woman.

ROBERT V. HATCHER, SR.

Old age doesn't seem so bad when you consider the alternative.

MAURICE CHEVALIER

Growing old is a slow march into enemy territory.

HENRY JAMES

If a young or middle-aged man, when leaving a company, does not recollect where he laid his hat, it is nothing; but if the

same inattention is discovered in an old man, people will shrug
up their shoulders and say, "His memory is going."

SAMUEL JOHNSON

One must wait until the evening to see how splendid the day
has been.

SOPHOCLES

When people tell you how young you look, they are also
telling you how old you are.

CARY GRANT

An interviewer asked John Barrymore if acting was as much
fun as it used to be. "Young man," said Barrymore, "I am seventy-five. Nothing is as much fun as it used to be."

If I'd known I was going to live this long, I'd have taken
better care of myself.

Anon.

Messenger: Sire, I have news.
King Osbert: Keep it. At my age, all news is bad.

One of the ironies of old age is that with time becoming shorter and more precious by the minute, you have to fritter away more and more of it on such trivialities as searching for your eyeglasses or for something else you had put down only a moment ago; on looking up telephone numbers you have called a dozen times a week for the past five years; on having prescriptions refilled, and on remembering to take your vitamin pills and to use your eyedrops; on attending funerals and writing letters of condolence; and on getting up in the middle of the night. Also, cuts and scratches take longer to heal.

I have decided that the heaviest penalty to old age—with the exception of fading eyesight, which spreads a veil over everything and makes it look as if it had been painted by J. M. W. Turner—the heaviest penalty is memory that fades as fast as vision. At first I tried to combat it by writing notes to myself, but I soon found that if I kept them overnight, my handwriting so contorted itself that the words might have been Bulgarian or Nahuatl, for all the information they conveyed. Result: a time-saving device became another time-waster.

You know you're getting old when you've got money to burn, but the fire's gone out.

HY GARDNER

—and when you look the food over, instead of the waitress.

IB.

The greatest time-saver I know is owning two pairs of eyeglasses.

Openers

I DON'T SAY that all the following opening lines are my favorites, but they are certainly among my most memorable.

In the beginning God created the heaven and the earth.
GENESIS 1:1

Casey Stengel naked was a sight to remember.
ROBERT W. CREAMYER,
Stengel: His Life and Times

At the open window of the great library of Blandings Castle, drooping like a wet sock as was his habit when he had nothing to prop his spine against, the Earl of Emsworth, that amiable and boneheaded peer, stood gazing out over his domain.
P. G. WODEHOUSE,
Leave It to Psmith

Case 126. B———, an Alsatian postman, early manifested intense excitement in the presence of bird-cages.

R. VON KRAFFT-EBING,
Psychopathia Sexualis

It was a dark and stormy night. . . .

EDWARD BULWER-LYTTON,
Paul Clifford

I need not say why and how, at the age of fifteen, I became the mistress of the Earl of Craven.

HARRIETTE WILSON,
Memoirs (1825)

It was not until several weeks after he had decided to murder his wife that Dr. Bickleigh took any active steps in the matter.

FRANCIS ILES,
Malice Aforethought

When I was, quoth Carpalin, a whoremaster at Orleans . . .

RABELAIS, *Gargantua and Pantagruel,*
Book III, Chapter 34

One dollar and eighty-seven cents. That was all. And sixty cents of it was in pennies.

O. HENRY, "The Gift of the Magi"

Note: It is impossible to make up $1.87 if sixty cents of it is in pennies.

Stately, plump Buck Mulligan came from the stairhead, bearing a bowl of lather on which a mirror and a razor lay crossed.

JAMES JOYCE, *Ulysses*

In a hole in the ground there lived a hobbit. Not a nasty, dirty, wet hole, filled with the ends of worms and an oozy smell, nor yet a dry, bare, sandy hole, with nothing in it to sit down on or to eat: it was a hobbit-hole, and that means comfort.

J. R. R. TOLKIEN, *The Hobbit*

192

Opinions of People
and Places

A DAY AWAY from Tallulah [Bankhead] is like a month in the country.

HOWARD DIETZ

Switzerland is a curst, selfish, swinish country of brutes, placed in the most romantic region in the world.

LORD BYRON

Swiss scenery is beautiful but dumb.

DOROTHY PARKER

I have just returned from Boston. It is the only thing to do, if you find yourself up there.

FRED ALLEN

Living in California adds ten years to a man's life. Those extra ten years I'd like to spend in New York.

HARRY RUBY

California: The west coast of Iowa.

JOAN DIDION

Maine is as dead, intellectually, as Abyssinia. Nothing is ever heard from it.

H. L. MENCKEN

Of course, America had often been discovered before, but it had been hushed up.

OSCAR WILDE

Switzerland is simply a large, humpy, solid rock, with a thin skin of grass stretched over it.

MARK TWAIN

Mae West. A plumber's idea of Cleopatra.

W. C. FIELDS

Geneva: Voltaire thought it "shining," Harriet Beecher Stowe, "lovely," Ruskin, "a bird's nest," Emerson, "stern," Dostoevski called it "horrible, ugly, rotten, expensive ... dull, gloomy, Protestant, stupid." (In fairness to Geneva, I should point out that Dostoevski was suffering from both hemorrhoids and epilepsy at the time of his visit.)

Ask the traveled inhabitant of any nation in what country on earth you would rather live? Certainly in my own ... Which would be your second choice? France.

THOMAS JEFFERSON, *Writings*

I would have loved France. Without the French.

D. H. LAWRENCE

Jenny Lind considered France so wicked that she sang there only once, at a charity concert in Nice.

If I owned Texas and Hell, I'd rent out Texas and live in Hell.

GEN. PHILIP SHERIDAN

A Texan was complaining to a telephone operator about the size of an item on his bill, "I could call Hell for less than that!" he protested.

"No doubt, sir," the operator said. "It's only a local call."

Miami Beach is where neon goes to die.

LENNY BRUCE

Marilyn Monroe. A vacuum with nipples.

OTTO PREMINGER

Philadelphia, a metropolis sometimes known as the City of Brotherly Love, but more accurately as the City of Bleak November Afternoons.

S. J. PERELMAN

First prize, one week in Philadelphia. Second prize, two weeks in Philadelphia.

JACK WHITE, of the Club Eighteen

I showed my appreciation of my native land in the usual Irish way: by getting out of it as soon as I possibly could.

GEORGE BERNARD SHAW

Los Angeles: A big hard-boiled city with no more personality than a paper cup.

RAYMOND CHANDLER

Los Angeles: Nineteen suburbs in search of a metropolis.

H. L. MENCKEN

Los Angeles is Bridgeport with palms.

BEN HECHT

There's nothing wrong with Southern California that a rise in the ocean level wouldn't cure.

ROSS MACDONALD

Hollywood, that flatulent cave of the winds.

JOHN BARRYMORE

There is a nimiety, a too-muchness, in the German people.

THOMAS CARLYLE

No one is so third-class as a second-class Englishman.

Anon.

Personal Descriptions
(CONT'D)

HE HAS FAULTS that make San Andreas look like a hairline crack.
Anon.

Maurice Bowra, an Oxford don, was famous for his hypersensitivity. He said of himself that he has "a skin too few."
ELIZABETH LONGFORD,
Condensed from *The Pebbled Shore*

Toss a hat at Katharine Hepburn, and wherever it hits, it will hang.
A Hollywood producer

The marks of [Nero's] horror and despair continued on his face after he was dead [at the age of thirty-one], his eyes staring in a most dreadful manner, to the affrighting of all beholders. . . . Nature had delineated his manners on his face and the whole of his body; for he had little eyes, and covered with fat, his throat

197

and chin joined together, a thick neck, a great belly, and his legs slender. All which proportions made him not unlike a swine, whose filthiness he well expressed. His chin turned upwards, which was a sign of his cruelty. Fair hair, small legs, and his face rather fair than majestical were pregnant signs of his effeminateness.

The Great Historical, Geographical and Poetical Dictionary (1694)

[My grandmother's youngest son] was thought to be the genius of the family. . . . I don't think he took a degree [at Balliol], but he at least achieved the manner and appearance of a don: small body, high forehead, short staccato utterance, followed by a knowing chuckle, and a pipe smoked with an air of portentous wisdom. He was the most completely futile human being I have ever met; he could not ride a bicycle or dig in the garden, and never seemed to read a book. His only visible occupation was to repaint used golf balls, which he picked up on the course.

KENNETH CLARK,
Another Part of the Wood

I'd as soon go to bed with a bicycle.

P. H., of a bony American beauty

He was so ugly not even the tide would go out with him.

C. D. B. BRYAN

[Gandolf was] a little old man with a tall pointed blue hat, a long grey cloak, a silver scarf over which a long white beard hung down below his waist, and immense black boots.

J. R. R. TOLKIEN, *The Hobbit*

[Dorothy Parker was] a little and extraordinarily pretty woman, with dark hair, a gentle apologetic smile and great reproachful eyes.

ALEXANDER WOOLLCOTT
Later he added that she was "a blend of Little Nell and Lady Macbeth."

Fred Allen's face might have been labeled "villainy's ledger." The avarice of a Scrooge, the treachery of a Quisling, the malignant cunning of a Fu Manchu—all were written there in an alphabet of pouches, squints and seams. . . . Like a gangster, he had a powder burn on his hand; a property man had been careless with a blank pistol. Like a stool pigeon's, his eyes were shifty and darting; he used to be a juggler, and most jugglers have darting eyes. Like a brawler, his teeth were chipped; one of his juggling stunts was to hold a fork in his mouth and spear turnips tossed from the audience. Withall, he was a kindly, devout Catholic who seldom drank, never gambled and quietly gave away far more money than he spent on himself.

> J. BRYAN, III, "Eighty Hours for a Laugh,"
> *Saturday Evening Post*

[Lina Cavalieri, the opera singer,] has the face of a siren and the eyes of a mermaid. Her sinuous curves fasten themselves into the memory and fire in the heart of the beholder a depth of passion hard to understand. All that women of her build and eye desire is to add new scalps to their belts.

> JOHN ARMSTRONG "Who's Lonely Now?" CHALONER,
> of his sister-in-law

Bernarr MacFadden had the wild glare of an educated horse doing a problem in arithmetic.

> ALVA JOHNSTON

Blackbeard [Captain Edward Teach] was accustomed to twist [his beard] up with ribbons, in small tails and turn them about his ears . . . which, his eyes naturally looking fierce and wild, made him altogether such a figure that imagination cannot form an idea of a Fury from hell to look more frightful.

> CAPTAIN CHARLES JOHNSON,
> *General History of Pirates,* 1725

John Randolph of Roanoke, the duelist and brilliant, witty statesman, stood six feet three, but measured only thirteen inches across the shoulders. Col. John S. Mosby, the dashing commander of the Virginia Partisan Rangers, weighed only 125 pounds. Gen. Robert E. Lee wore a size 6 shoe.

> Legree he sported a brass-buttoned coat,
> A snake-skin necktie, a blood-red shirt.

199

Legree he had a beard like a goat,
And a thick hairy neck, and eyes like dirt.
His puffed-out cheeks were fish-belly white,
He had great long teeth, and an appetite.
He ate raw meat, 'most every meal,
And rolled his eyes till the cat would squeal.

VACHEL LINDSAY, "Simon Legree"

As an associate editor of the *Saturday Evening Post* some fifty
years ago—the OLD *Post*, I hasten to state—I had to read some
twenty or more short stories a day, plus several novels. Sometimes it seemed as if I were reading the same one over and over
again. All the heroines had "sherry-colored eyes," and the
breezes "liked to toy with the tendrils of their taffy-colored
hair," whereas the heroes' hair "curled crisply at their temples,"
and their eyelids "crinkled when they smiled."

I don't know what the style in heroes and heroines is today.
I gave up reading magazine fiction long ago.

Oscar Wilde was a mixture of Apollo and a monster.

GEORGE MEREDITH

Talleyrand is a silk stocking filled with mud.

NAPOLEON

SYDNEY SMITH, of Macaulay: "A book in breeches."
MACAULAY, of Horace Walpole: "A heartless fribble."
WALPOLE, of Lady Mary Wortley Montagu: "An old, foul, taw-
dry, painted, plastered personage."

Of a lady of fashion: If she cut her finger, she'd insist on
having it dressed by Yves Saint-Laurent.

Mama says that [Jane Austen] was the prettiest, silliest, most
affected, husband-hunting butterfly she ever remembered.

CHARLOTTE BRONTË

[Greta Garbo was] a deer in the body of a woman, living
resentfully in the Hollywood zoo.

CLARE BOOTHE LUCE

He has no more personality than the state of West Virginia.

Anon.

[Katharine Hepburn] had a face that belongs to the sea and the wind, with large rockinghorse nostrils and teeth that you just know bite an apple every day.

CECIL BEATON

Count Boni de Castellane is an unwieldy person, with little pig's eyes set in a wide expanse of pasty-hued face.

TUROT, a journalist in Lausanne

Lucius Beebe dubbed Count Boni "the diminutive mooch."

I asked a burly friend of mine how his even burlier brother was doing. "No change," he said. "Still wears a size six hat and a twenty-two collar."

An elderly black woman in Gloucester County, Virginia, explained a neighborhood boy, weak-witted from in-breeding, as "He too close kin to hisself."

George Sand had a great soul and a perfectly enormous bottom.

CHARLES AUGUSTIN SAINTE-BEUVE

Under a forehead roughly comparable to that of Javanese and Piltdown man are visible a pair of tiny pig eyes, lit up alternately by greed and concupiscence.

S. J. PERELMAN, of himself

[Calvin Coolidge,] that runty, aloof little man who quacks through his nose when he speaks.

WILLIAM ALLEN WHITE

Prophets without Honor

(CONT'D)

No MATTER WHAT HAPPENS, the U.S. Navy is not going to be caught napping.

SECRETARY OF THE NAVY FRANK KNOX,
on December 5, 1941

Heavier-than-air flying machines are impossible.

LORD KELVIN, British physicist, 1895

My imagination refuses to see any sort of submarine doing anything but suffocate its crew and founder at sea.

H. G. WELLS

Airplanes are interesting toys, but have no military value.

MARSHAL FERDINAND FOCH, 1911

Louis XVI's entry in his diary for July 14, 1789, was "Nothing." This was the day that the mob stormed the Bastille.

Because of the greatness of the Shah, Iran is an island of stability in the Middle East.

PRESIDENT JIMMY CARTER

The world will little note nor long remember what we say here.

ABRAHAM LINCOLN,
"Gettysburg Address"

I will never marry again.

BARBARA HUTTON, after divorcing the second of what would be her seven husbands

When Louis B. Mayer, the head of MGM, was considering a bid for the screen rights to *Gone with the Wind*, his chief lieutenant, Irving Thalberg, told him, "Forget it, Louis! No Civil War picture ever made a nickel."

I have no political ambitions for myself or my children.

JOSEPH P. KENNEDY

203

Democracy is finished in England.

IB., 1940

This country couldn't run without Prohibition. This is the industrial fact.

HENRY FORD, 1929

With over 50 foreign cars already on sale here, the Japanese auto industry isn't likely to carve out a big slice of the U.S. market.

Business Week, 1979

Stocks have reached what looks like a permanently high plateau.

ECONOMIST IRVING FISHER
October 17, 1929
The market crashed on October 29, Black Tuesday.

A drama coach, to a young girl named Lucille Ball: "Forget it, miss. You're wasting your time and mine."

HY GARDNER

Puns
(CONT'D)

LEIGH HUNT (1784–1850) was the first on record to pull the tulips/two lips pun.

Sign over the urinals in the Players Club, New York:

THE MORE HASTE
THE LESS PEED

Have you noticed how often rich people run to corpulence? You could call it an illustration of the theory of conspicuous waist.

Anon.

Two brothers started a cattle ranch and asked their mother to suggest a name for it. " 'Focus,' " she suggested. "Because it's where the sons raise meat."

This was said to be the only perfect triple pun in our language, until Clifton Fadiman came up with another: He had caught the fancy of a notoriously available young woman who was relentless in her pursuit. "It's a case," he explained to a friend, "where the tail dogs the wag."

And one more triple, although this one is rather artificial, and you can hear the machinery of contrivance creak:

A Dutch sailor was so bullied by the bucko mate that when their freighter tied up at Yokohama, he jumped ship. As do so many Dutchmen, he had a green thumb, and he soon found a pleasant job tending the gardens at the famous Shinto shrine in Nara. Before long his skill was known all over Japan, and other gardeners came to consult him. Then the great hurricane of 1921 struck, uprooting many of his flowers and covering his lawns with salt water and mud. He started restoring them at once, and he was hard at work again when a new group of gardeners came to Nara to see him.

"Where is the Master?" they asked the gatekeeper.

He said, "Mynheer is re-seeding at the temples."

When Winston Churchill lost his seat in Parliament, someone telegraphed him, "What good is a W.C. without a seat?"

[In the middle quarters of this century,] New York had punsters aplenty, like George Kaufman ("One man's Mede is another man's Persian") and Franklin Pierce Adams (FPA) ("Take care of the peonies, and the dahlias will take care of themselves"). Corey Ford once wrote me from Bangkok, "I just ran into a fraternity Buddha of mine. I recognized him by his old school Thai." Ford may not have ranked among the master paronomasiasts, but on anybody's punning team, he'd have been a good utility outfielder. I rest my case on his sobriquet for Frank Sullivan, when they were sharing an apartment: "Ford's ugly roomer."

J. BRYAN, III, *Merry Gentlemen (and One Lady)*

Kaufman, FPA, Ford, Dorothy Parker, Oliver Herford, Marc Connelly—all are gone now, alas!, but one of the masters remains: Clifton Fadiman, who won his degree as M.P. (Master Paronomasiast) with the triple pun I quoted several paragraphs ago. Here are a few more to nail down the title:

He was heard to remark at a wine tasting, "The quality of Meursault is not strained" and, a moment later, "Throw this poor dog a Beaune." He once protested that his wife was running a free-lunch counter for every stray cat in the neighborhood—"a sort of alleycatessen." Mrs. F. herself complained that a bed of drooping shastas in their garden looked "lackadaisical." But my favorite of Fadiman's has to be spoken. He is waiting, he says, for someone to ask him where to buy a pint of camel's milk. His answer is all ready: "At the nearest dromedairy."

Sir Shane Leslie preserves a nice double pun in an anecdote about a certain Lord Erne, who was notorious for his interminable anecdotes, and his lady, who "waggled her bosom." Sir Shane presupposes your acquaintance with Gray's "Elegy," when he writes that the noble couple were known as "the storied Erne and animated bust."

During the Marianas Turkey Shoot in June 1944, an American Navy officer, a veteran of Guadalcanal, New Georgia, and Bougainville, remarked, "The Solomons in all their glory had not a raid like one of these!"

When young Dr. "Willie" Wilmer of Washington, D.C., who would eventually become a world-famous oculist, was considering where to open his first office, he consulted his father, Bishop Richard H. Wilmer. The bishop dearly loved a pun and seldom missed a chance to make one. Now he said, "My son, there are only two possible addresses for an oculist in Washington: C Street and I Street."

Dr. Wilmer actually hung out his shingle on I Street.

Hanging is too good for a man who makes puns; he should be drawn and quoted.

FRED ALLEN

Put-Downs
(CONT'D)

ON ELECTION NIGHT in 1916, the Republican nominee for the Presidency, Charles Evans Hughes, retired to bed in full confidence that he had defeated the Democratic nominee, President Woodrow Wilson. However, the late returns showed that Wilson had pulled 277 electoral votes to Hughes's 254. A reporter on his way to inform Mr. Hughes was intercepted by a member of the staff, who told him, "The President is asleep and must not be disturbed. Would you care to leave a message for him?"

The reporter said, "Yeah. Tell the President he ain't President."

Prince Philip, Duke of Edinburgh, conversing with a Brazilian admiral, asked if he had won his gallery of medals in battles on the artificial lake at Brasilia, his country's new capital.

The admiral's cold, crushing reply was, "At least I didn't get them for marrying my wife!"

Groucho Marx, to a pestilential bore: "I never forget a face, but in your case I'll try to make an exception."

And Fred Allen to another such: "How much would you charge to haunt a house?"

To Daniel O'Connell's comment that he was a Jew, Disraeli retorted, "Yes, I am a Jew, and when the ancestors of the right honourable gentleman were brutal savages in an unknown island, mine were priests in the temple of Solomon."

Lord Leighton, president of the Royal Academy and painter of neoclassical scenes, once asked Whistler why he never bothered to finish any of his paintings. Whistler asked Leighton, "Why do you ever bother to start yours?"

A rear admiral reporting for duty at the Pentagon went to "make his number" with the formidable Chief of Naval Operations, Adm. Ernest J. King. On his way out, he stopped in the anteroom to put in an urgent long-distance call. The connection was poor, and he had to shout. King heard him and barked at his flag lieutenant, "What the hell's going on out there?"
"The admiral is talking with New York, sir."
"Well, tell him to use the goddam phone!"

Another of King's put-downs:
He was a maneater who liked to munch little ensigns, raw, for appetizers, then dine on plump young lieutenants. One such lieutenant, Arthur Robbins, a friend of mine, told me this story:
The Navy had assigned him to the Motion Picture Section of the Public Relations Division, where he was informed that his main duty would be to show gun-camera films to Admiral King. A number of the Navy's fighter planes had cameras mounted in their wings. When the pilot pushed the button to fire his guns, the cameras "fired" too, and because they were focused on the point where the streams of bullets converged, the films were often highly dramatic. King enjoyed them so richly that he gave orders for all new gun-camera films to be shown him *at once*, even at the cost of interrupting a high-brass conference. Arthur Robbins' job was to rush these films to Admiral King's office

and run them off. When they were over, he'd say, "That's all for today, Admiral," and King would dismiss his with, "Thank you, Jones."

Several months of this almost daily "Jones" routine exasperated Arthur until he finally mustered his nerve and protested, "My name isn't Jones, Admiral. It's Robbins."

King pelted him with the two pieces of gravel he used for eyes. "Very well, Jones," he said.

The Yale Corporation, which governs the university, was discussing whether to make one of the sciences a compulsory course. Sen. Robert A. Taft remarked that he had never taken a science course. Secretary of State Dean Acheson commented, "The defense rests."

NORMAN HICKMAN

One of the most famous put-downs in the chronicles of American politics was scored at a banquet in New York, with President Taft as the guest of honor and the witty Chauncey Depew as toastmaster. Mr. Taft was grossly obese, but he never took offense at gibes about his figure. One of them came now:

Depew gestured toward Mr. Taft's paunch and remarked in a piercing stage whisper that Washington gossips were murmuring "pregnancy." He went on, "If they are correct, and if the baby is a boy, I trust that our patriotic President will name it 'Sam,' for Uncle Sam. And if it's a girl, 'Columbia.'"

President Taft broke in: "And if it's only gas, as I know it is, I'll name it 'Chauncey Depew.'" ·

A new member, young, of a stodgy London club, made his nervous entrance one evening and was surprised and relieved to have an elderly curmudgeon beckon to him. He did not speak to the expectant youngster, but merely scrutinized his costume, at painful length—tweed suit, brown shoes, flannel shirt, woolen necktie—which was in truth a trifle informal for the august halls. At length the old boy said coldly, "Taking the night train to Scotland, I see," and retired behind his newspaper.

A certain English novelist of the early 1900s married a potful of money, including a country mansion, and thereupon became

211

rather more patronizing than his old friends enjoyed. He greeted one of them in their London club and invited him down for a weekend at "The Towers."

"Delighted!" the friend said. "What number?"

You're a good example of why some animals eat their young.
JIM SAMUELS to a heckler, quoted by Robert Byrne in *The Other 637 Best Things Anybody Ever Said*

Quiz

1. QUESTION: Who is the odd-man-out in this list? Washington, Jefferson, Franklin, Lincoln, Jackson, Grant, McKinley, Cleveland, Theodore Roosevelt.
   Answer: Roosevelt. All the others have their portraits on U.S. banknotes.

2. Question: How many men have walked on the moon?
   Answer: Twelve: Armstrong, Aldrin, Conrad, Bean, Shepard, Scott, Irwin, Mitchell, Young, Duke, Cernan, Schmitt.

3. Question: Who was first called the Father of His Country?
   Answer: Cicero.

4. Question: Unwrap the paper spiral on a china-marking pencil, and how long is the strip?
   Answer: 434.5 inches, or 36.2 feet.

5. Question: How old was Captain John Smith when he helped found the colony at Jamestown in 1607?
Answer: He was twenty-six when he sailed from London in December 1606, and twenty-seven when he landed the following spring.

6. Question: How old was Salome when she danced before Herod and demanded the head of John the Baptist as her fee?
Answer: When the playwright Philip Barry was researching for his play *Salome* (never produced), he estimated that she was fourteen.

7. Question: Who founded the British Empire, by establishing the first English possession outside Europe, and when and where?
Answer: Sir Humphrey Gilbert (Sir Walter Raleigh's half-brother) established a colony at what is now St. John's, Newfoundland, in 1583.

8. Question: Where is Sir Winston Churchill buried—in St. Paul's or Westminster Abbey?
Answer: In neither; he is buried next to his father and mother in the churchyard at Bladon, near Blenheim Palace, where he was born.

NORMAN HICKMAN

9. Question: The tower that houses Big Ben has four clock faces. From ground level to the clock faces is what proportion of the total height of the tower: Half? Two thirds? Three quarters? Two fifths?
Answer: The height of the tower is 316 feet, and the centers of the dials are at 180 feet, or not quite three fifths (189 feet) of the way up.

Religion
(CONT'D)

ALTHOUGH ISTANBUL has a huge and magnificent museum (formerly a basilica) of Saint Sophia, there was never any such saint. "Sophia" means "wisdom" in Greek, and since the words for "saint" and "holy" are the same in Greek, the correct name for the edifice is Holy Wisdom.

An angel whose muscles developed no more power weight-for-weight than those of an eagle or a pigeon would require a breast projecting about four feet to house the muscles engaged in working its wings, while to economize in weight, its legs would have to be reduced to mere stilts.

J. B. S. HALDANE,
"On Being the Right Size"

God seems to have left the receiver off the hook, and time is running out.

ARTHUR KOESTLER

215

I cannot believe in a God who wants to be praised all the time.

FRIEDRICH WILHELM NIETZSCHE

The cosmos is a gigantic flywheel making 10,000 revolutions a minute. Man is a sick fly taking a dizzy ride on it. Religion is the theory that the wheel was designed and set spinning to give him the ride.

H. L. MENCKEN

Augustus Carp, Esq., by Himself, mentions his regular attendance at the church of St. James the Less in London; and later at St. James the Lesser Still; and ultimately at St. James-the-Least-of-All. Whether these churches actually exist, I don't know. But I do know of a Church of the Good Shepherd which its disappointed congregation came to think of as "the Church of the Pretty Good Shepherd." And I know another church, built with a handsome bequest by a notorious libertine. Never mind its formal name; it is popularly known as the Church of the Atonement.

Religion's in the heart, not in the knees.

DOUGLAS JERROLD

There is but one God—is it Allah or Jehovah? The palm tree is sometimes called the date tree, but there is only one tree.

BENJAMIN DISRAELI

The country with the largest Catholic population is Brazil with 121 million.

An agnostic of my acquaintance excused his nonattendance at services by saying that his father had lost his hair by sitting in damp churches, and that therefore . . .

Did you hear of the parson who began his sermon, "As God said—and rightly—"? It grows on you.

RUPERT HART-DAVIS

Heaven and Hell:

Hell is an unending church service without God. Heaven is God without a church service.

In hell the only two kinds of music are Muzak and Disco.

In hell the auto mechanics have to drive the cars they "fixed" on earth.

In heaven no one ever gets drunk, but everyone drinks. In hell you get hangovers without even drinking.

PETER KREFT,
A Turn of the Clock

Harry Cooper was driving his small son through one of the Virginia suburbs of Washington, D.C.

"Daddy, what's this town?"

"Falls Church."

"Where's True Church, Daddy?"

The fourth-century chapel of St. Quirinus, in Luxembourg City, has room for only three pews, but because the pulpit has two "exposures," the priest can address at the same time the overflow congregation standing outside.

217

It is widely believed that "IHS" are the initials of "Iesus Hominum Savior" (Jesus Savior of Men), or of "In Hoc Signo" (In This Sign [you will conquer]), or "In Hoc Salus" (In This Salvation). They represent none of these, but are the symbol of Jesus, from ΙΗΣΟΥΣ (Iēsous), his name in Greek capitals.

Cove Creek, Virginia, is the home of the Independent Missionary Fundamental Premillennial Charity Baptist Church.

Why should we take advice on sex from the Pope? If he knows anything about it, he shouldn't.

GEORGE BERNARD SHAW

Even in the valley of the shadow of death, two and two do not make six.

LEO TOLSTOY, when urged to return to the Russian Orthodox Church.

The final item in the category "Religion" in *Hodgepodge* is this: "I know men, and I tell you that Jesus Christ was not a man."

Napoleon to Beauterne, on St. Helena

I had not been able to identify "Beauterne," so I asked readers to help. They did. The correct name is "General Henri Gratien Bertrand."

Royalty

(CONT'D)

QUEEN MARIA I of Portugal married her uncle, Dom Pedro. Their son, João, at sixteen married his aunt, Princess Maria. She and João had no son, so they obtained a dispensation for their daughter to marry her uncle.

King Edward VII used to visit the Hotel du Palais at Biarritz every year from early March to late April. He traveled incognito, as "the Duke of Lancaster," but his identity must have been fairly obvious since he brought with him two aides-de-camp, two secretaries, a doctor, a nurse, a courier, a private detective, a chief valet and eight assistants, a chauffeur, a mechanic, and a man from Scotland Yard. (The mechanic's job was to keep the royal Mercedes in repair; the Yard man's was to break impertinent cameras with his umbrella.) His Majesty's retinue also included a favorite dog, Caesar, and a favorite lady, Mrs. Keppel. Queen Alexandra usually stayed home.

Of all the Palace/Palais/Palazzo Hotels in the world, only the Palais in Biarritz was actually a palace: Emperor Napoleon III and Empress Eugénie's.

There are more statues of Queen Victoria in Montreal than in any other place in the world.

Caroline, the uncrowned queen of England's King George IV, attended a ball in Geneva in 1820 naked to the waist, and "displaying a bosom of more than ample proportions."

Second only to Queen Elizabeth II herself, the star attraction in her coronation procession was the massive Queen of Tonga, riding in an open carriage with her diminutive Foreign Minister beside her. Someone asked, "Who's he?"
Noel Coward said, "Her lunch."

Kings and queens are only secondarily fathers and mothers.
THE DUKE OF WINDSOR

In Russian Georgia, the title "prince" is roughly equivalent to "mister" in America.

WESTBROOK PEGLER

Mr. Hansell, tutor to the young Prince of Wales (later King Edward VIII) and his brother the Duke of York (later King George VI), was asked what was the most important thing to teach a young man. His answer was, "Teach him not to be clever." (An anonymous courtier once remarked, "The trouble with the Princes is too much Hansell and not enough Gretel.")

The coronation ceremony of Empress Elisabeth of Austria-Hungary required her to be anointed in her right armpit.

Buckingham Palace has 1½ miles of corridors, 160 clocks, 230 servants, 600 rooms, 2,000 electric light bulbs, and 10,000 pieces of furniture.

By King Edward VII's order, the clocks at the Royal Family's country estate, Sandringham, were kept an hour ahead of time, to compensate for Queen Alexandra's incurable tardiness. King George V continued the practice, but one of King Edward VIII's first acts after his accession was to have the clocks reset to the correct time.

The Sexes
(CONT'D)

OLD BOYS have their playthings as well as the young ones; the difference is only in the price.

BENJAMIN FRANKLIN,
Poor Richard's Almanac

The man's desire is for the woman; but the woman's desire is rarely other than for the desire of the man.

SAMUEL TAYLOR COLERIDGE, *Table Talk*

Fireblood . . . began to take her by the hand, and proceeded so warmly . . . he in a few minutes ravished the fair creature, or at least would have ravished her, if she had not, by a timely compliance, prevented him.

HENRY FIELDING, *Jonathan Wild*

As the old Countess of Essex said when asked at *eighty* by a young jackanapes: "When does a woman have done with love?", "Ask someone older than me!"

JANE WELSH CARLYLE, *Letters*

(*Jackanapes* is an interesting word; some say it means "a monkey from Naples," *jack* or *jocko* being the generic pet name for a monkey, as *puss* is for a cat, *bossy* for a cow, and so on.)

To succeed with the opposite sex, tell her you're impotent. She can't wait to disprove it.

CARY GRANT

No one will ever win the battle of the sexes; there's too much fraternizing with the enemy.

HENRY KISSINGER

A woman was being rehearsed for a TV interview on her one-hundredth birthday. The MC said, "You look in good health, madam. Tell me: were you ever bedridden?"

"Hundreds of times!" the old girl said. "And once in a buggy. But you can't say that on the air!"

A promiscuous person is someone who is getting more sex than you are.

Said of a notorious swordsman: "His rutting season begins on October first and runs straight through to the end of September."

D.F.

An archaeologist is the best husband a woman can have: the older she gets, the more he is interested in her.

AGATHA CHRISTIE, who married an
archaeologist, Sir Max Mallowan

Marriage is popular because it combines the maximum of temptation with the maximum of opportunity.

GEORGE BERNARD SHAW

A mistress should be like a little country retreat near the town, not to dwell in constantly, but for a night away.

WILLIAM WYCHERLEY
The Country Wife

In the duel of sex, woman fights from a dreadnaught, and man from an open raft.

H. L. MENCKEN

Virgin derives from the Latin *vir*, "a man," and *gin*, "a trap."

Anon.

Similes from the Boondocks

(CONT'D)

As CALM AS A WIDDER-WOMAN at her third wedding.

"STEEP" HILL

Trapped like a fart in a mitten.

Panama City, Florida

He was busier than an octopus going through a revolving door.

FRED ALLEN

Jack Benny's arm looks like a buggy whip with fingers.

IB.

His desk looks like the floor of a hillbilly's privy.

IB.

As unobtrusive as a sow in a synagogue.

FREDERICK FORSYTH,
The Fourth Protocol

As helpless as a nun in a high wind.

Anon.

Being welcomed by an affectionate Labrador is like going through a car-wash in a convertible with the top down.

Anon.

As flat behind as a tame bee.

COUSIN CHARLIE PAGE (none of us in the family ever knew what this meant)

As popular as a wet dog at a cotillion.

As smooth as the inside of the school-marm's leg.

W. H. M.

As fat as a tick.

Guinea, Virginia

As scarce as corsets in a Gypsy camp.

ABE MARTIN

As much chance as a balloon in a cloudburst of pitchforks.

NEAL O'HARA

She clung to him like a label.

CHARLES COLLINS

As infectious as a yawn.

Baltimore

A lawyer as slippery as a watermelon seed.

Jackson, Mississippi

All screwed up, like Hogan's nanny-goat.

U. S. Navy

Screwed up like a Chinese fire-drill.

IB.

226

Similes from the Boondocks

He danced like a man with arthritis setting up a deck chair.

I loved him like a brothel.

S. J. PERELMAN

As mean as a junkyard dog.

Richmond

She blushed like an apple tree in autumn.

Anon.

Sleep

PIERRE FLUCHAIRE has written a book, *Bien Dormir pour Mieux Vivre* ("Sleep Well to Live Better"), advocating that everyone sleep less—as little as four hours a night. Salvador Dali, Isaac Asimov, Pavarotti, and Jacques Chirac are practitioners.

A number of great discoveries were hit upon during the night, Fluchaire points out. Dreaming, Einstein discovered relativity; Fleming found penicillin; Rutherford understood the constitution of the atom; Gauss formulated the laws of induction; Mendel revealed the laws of heredity, and Mozart composed *The Magic Flute.*

In the animal kingdom, one observes that certain animals apparently don't sleep at all—whales, antelopes, shrews, giraffes, wild elephants. Among fish, mullet. Albatrosses fly for thirty to fifty days without resting. A cow sleeps only about forty minutes in twenty-hours.

A Cuban, Tomás Izquierdo, fifty-three years old, hasn't slept

228

for forty-one years. Saint Colette slept only one hour every eight days. Saint Agatha of the Cross went without sleep the last eight years of her life. Saint Lidwine "knew only three hours of sleep in thirty years." Virgil, Horace, Churchill, Napoleon, Edison, Shaw, all slept less than five hours a night. Benjamin Franklin slept only two. Truman and Kennedy slept very little.

Edison said, "People eat twice too much and sleep twice too long."

Le Figaro, September 20, 1986

And presently the eyes closed, the muscles relaxed, the breathing became soft and regular, and sleep which does something that has slipped my mind to the something sleeve of care poured over me in a healing wave.

P. G. WODEHOUSE,
The Code of the Woosters

A person can stay awake for no longer than twelve days without permanent damage.

DR. BERNARD L. FRANKEL,
National Institute of Mental Health

Silly euphemism: "Sleep" with someone.

In the year 1546, William Foxley, potmaker for the Mint in the Tower of London, fell asleep, and continued sleeping, and could not be wakened [for] . . . fourteen days and fifteen nights or more. The cause of his thus sleeping could not be known, though the same was diligently searched after by the King's physicians, and other learned men.

JOHN SNOW, Survey of London

Kipling wrote a moving poem about insomnia, "The Merciful Town." I wanted to quote some of it here, but his estate charges too much.

Small Comforts and Satisfactions
(CONT'D)

ONE OF THE PLEASURES of reading old letters is the knowledge that they need no answer.

LORD BYRON

Falling asleep on a frosty night, to the soft crackling of a fire in the bedroom grate.

As a child, receiving one's first telegram or one's first long-distance call.

One of the secrets of a happy life is continuous small treats, and if some of these can be inexpensive and quickly procured, so much the better.

IRIS MURDOCH, *The Sea, the Sea*

Small Men

(CONT'D)

CAN YOU NAME seven famous small men? See end of this section.

Take three adults of the same scant inches, and one may be a midget, the second a Pygmy, and the third a dwarf. Pygmies belong to special races of mankind, dark-skinned and primitive. Their average height is less than five feet, but they are not malformed. Their parents were Pygmies, and their children will be Pygmies.

Dwarfs are common to all races. They are born dwarfs, with torsos normal or nearly so, but with short, thick, malformed limbs. Their parents were normal, and their children will be normal.

Midgets are also common to all races—commoner than is generally believed; there are perhaps 2,000 of them scattered around the world. They are not born midgets; they are normal at birth and for several years afterward. And they are not malformed; their proportions are almost perfect. Their parents were normal, and their children will be normal.

"He was so small, the only job he could get was as an engineer for a Lionel train."

Head bartender at P. J. Clarke's

Charles I of England stood only 4 feet 7 inches, even before his head was cut off. Croesus was a midget. Midas was a dwarf. Alexander Pope was only 4 feet 6. James Madison, the smallest of our Presidents, was described as "no bigger than half a piece of soap." Attila the Hun, "the Scourge of God," was a dwarf, standing just over 4 feet. Thutmose I, the warrior Pharaoh, was exactly 5 feet.

"You know, of course, that Jesus Christ was only four feet eleven," Robert Graves told me, then added, "He was lame and had red hair. He went to Rome in 41 and is buried in India—but you know all this."

David Ritchie, the original of Sir Walter Scott's *Black Dwarf,* was about three feet and a half. His skull, which was of an oblong and rather unusual shape, was of such strength that he could strike it with ease through the panel of a door or the end of a tar barrel. His laugh is said to have been quite horrible; and his screech-owl voice, shrill, uncouth and dissonant, corresponded well with his other peculiarities. He never wore shoes, being unable to adapt them to his misshaped feet. His habits indicated a mind sufficiently congenial to its uncouth tabernacle.

Waverley Anecdotes

Fiction abounds in small men. They are especially plentiful in fairy tales—Hop o' My Thumb, for instance, Little Jack Horner, and the nasty little King of Id, and Stuart Little, in E. B. White's book of that name. But probably the most famous small men of all are Doc, Grumpy, Sneezy, Dopey, Happy, Sleepy, and Bashful. The whole world knows them, thanks to Walt Disney's genius, and they will live forever.

Smells

(CONT'D)

PERFUME MANUFACTURERS URGE USERS to renew the scent on the "pulse points" of the body every four hours.

A frightened sheep exudes a smell so pungent and powerful that it will linger in the area for days.

"Coco" Chanel believed that 5 was her lucky number. Accordingly, she named her perfume "Number 5" and put it on sale on May 5—the fifth day of the fifth month—in 1921.

CHARLES PANATI
Extraordinary Origins of Ordinary Things

Perfumers bewilder me. Why do they name one of their brands "Cobra"? And another "Scoundrel"? And "Poison" and "Insolent"? Isn't the purpose of a perfume to charm, soothe, inspire, attract? What sort of man would be attracted by a perfume called "Insolent"? Perhaps Groucho Marx?

The best way to understand a foreign country is by its smell.

T. S. ELIOT

[Marcel Proust was "virtually persecuted" by perfume.] "My dear friend," he would say, "shall I be causing you much inconvenience if I ask you to take the handkerchief out of your jacket? You know how I can't stand perfume." And he gave three rings on the bell.

"Celeste [he told the maid], take the gentleman's handkerchief and put it in another room.—My dear friend, the last time you were so good as to come and see me . . . I was obliged to take the chair you sat in and keep it out in the courtyard for three days; it was impregnated with scent."

LÉON PIERRE-QUINT, *Marcel Proust: His Life and Work*

We each have an odor; our environment smells and our culture positively reeks. At the pit of the problem lie the apocrine glands, associated with underarm and genital hair, which get excited when we're frightened or aroused. . . . Men have more and larger apocrine glands than women, blacks more than Caucasians, and Caucasians more than Orientals. In fact, the Japanese, who use fewer cover-up perfumes and deodorants than

236

most nations, invented the aerosol air-freshener to fumigate the room after a Westerner had left.

DR. WILLIAM TAYLOR, olfactory expert

The poet Schiller kept rotting apples in his desk; their smell inspired him to composition.

Smiles

(CONT'D)

MOLOTOV HAS A SMILE like the Siberian winter.

WINSTON CHURCHILL

In vain Stamfordham [King George V's private secretary] begged him to display in public some of the geniality which delighted guests at his own table. "We sailors," the King replied, "never smile on duty."

KENNETH ROSE, *King George V*

One may smile, and smile, and be a villain.

SHAKESPEARE, *Hamlet*

Oh, sir, she smiled, no doubt
Whene'er I passed her; but who passed without
Much the same smile? This grew; I gave commands;
Then all smiles stopped together.

ROBERT BROWNING, "My Last Duchess"

238

Snobs

(CONT'D)

WILLIAM FAULKNER was asked in 1957 why he had consented to serve as writer-in-residence at the University of Virginia. "Because I like your country, Virginia, and Virginians," Faulkner said. "Virginians are snobs. I like snobs. A snob spends so much time being a snob, he has none left to bother other people."

Lord Wimbirne was a snob in reverse. When he gave one of his brilliant balls, he had the labels soaked off all the bottles of champagne, so that his guests could not see what a noble and expensive vintage it was.

THE DUKE OF WINDSOR, quoted in J. Bryan, III and Charles J. V. Murphy, *The Windsor Story*

Social Maxims

(CONT'D)

ADLAI STEVENSON'S MOTHER told him, "You can be either witty or popular, my son, but you can't be both."

Moderation in all things, especially in moderation.

Anon.

If you want to bring on a sneeze, picture an electric bulb lighting up. If you want to suppress one, picture a cow.

Anon.

XYZ: Examine Your Zipper.

Don't discuss anything with the monkey while the organ-grinder is in the room.

WINSTON CHURCHILL

Frank Costello, the late expatriate gangster, said he owed his long life to three maxims. The first was, "Always eat a large

breakfast." The second was, "Never try to cheat on your taxes."
He forbore to mention the third, an adjuration perhaps to avoid
sitting with one's back to a window.

MURRAY KEMPTON, The Richmond News Leader

A man is asking for trouble when he marries the only child
of very rich parents.

Anon.

The meek shall inherit the grandchildren.

GILBERT C. GREENWAY

I have never heard of a yachting party that did not end with
at least one broken friendship.

KENNETH CLARK,
Another Part of the Wood

He was a master of evasion, and gave us the good advice,
"Always pretend to have left your engagement book behind."

IB.

Be sure that your first meeting with a new acquaintance takes
place at *his* club, *his* restaurant, or *his* house. Then, if things go
sour, you can leave with a minimum of embarrassment.

Flies spread disease. Keep yours zipped.

Anon.

Never say you met a lady *on* the street. 'Er brother might 'ear you. Always say you met her *in* the street.

ROSA LEWIS of the Cavendish Hotel

"Be very careful o' widders all your life, 'specially if they've kept a public house."

CHARLES DICKENS, *Pickwick Papers*: Tony Weller to his son, Sam

The secret of success is to know something nobody else knows.

ARISTOTLE ONASSIS

When someone calls me "Comrade," I always put my hands in my pockets.

JAMES SEXTON, M.P.

When you're in a hotel in a strange town and are wishing for companionship, play the mezzanines! There's a woman at every desk, writing home to tell hubby how lonely she is. It's a setup!

R.K.

You've dropped your wife off at the airport, and you're about to drive home and smarten up for an off-limits date. *Wait a bit!* I beg you, *wait a bit!* Wait till her plane is airborne and on its way. Too many flights are scrubbed at the last minute, leaving too many husbands to find themselves in the pickle barrel.

IB.

My boy, make sure you marry a lady, and preferably one of your own religion. If you happen to love her, so much the better.

J. BRYAN I

Sport

(CONT'D)

IN THE THIRD ROUND of the 1959 Bing Crosby golf tournament, one pro played a par-3 hole in nineteen. And in the final round of the 1988 Bob Hope Classic, another pro five-putted a green. *Five putts!* Fellow duffers, take heart!

America's only ten-goal polo team was made up of Thomas Hitchcock, Jr., Michael G. Phipps, Steward B. Iglehart, and Cecil Smith. When this dream team beat the British for the championship, Bob Considine, the sports-writer, began his account thus: "Yankee Doodle went to town today, riding on a pony."

Professional golf contributes more to charity than all other sports combined—$17.6 million in 1987.

Sententious young prig that I was, I once remarked to my father, "I like a good loser."
Father said, "I like any kind of loser."

A field goal in football—snap, reception, placement, kick—takes one and one-fifth seconds.

STUART A. SANDOW, *Durations*

Composite account of a college football game, as written by sports reporters of the 1920s:

Campus surrenders to fair invaders ... Annual Turkey Day grid classic ... Stands a riot of color ... Emotions running high ... Opposing captains meet in midfield ... Coin flashes in October sunlight ... Heads! ... Referee: "May best team win!" ... Line up ... Whistle shrills ... INSERTNAME's toe meets pigskin with resounding thump ... Game is on ... Plucky little quarterback barks signals ... Fullback a veritable tower of strength ... Halfbacks weaving, bobbing, dodging ... Score tied ... Purple shadows draw in ... Final, supreme effort in shadow of goalposts ... Touchdown! ... Well earned victory for the INSERTCOLORS.

My late mother-in-law, Mrs. B., an excellent wing shot, was invited on a turkey drive in Georgia. The guns were posted along a straight road that ran through a pine woods, and the beaters drove the birds toward them. The great ventriloquist Edgar Bergen was on Mrs. B.'s right. A moment after they had taken their positions, a high bird came over. Both fired, and the bird fell dead between them.

Bergen called, "Nice shot!"

"Thanks," Mrs. B. called back, "but it's your bird!"

Bergen protested, but Mrs. B. was firm: Bergen had killed the turkey. They argued until Bergen finally said, "Wait a minute. I can settle it." He picked up the dead bird's head. "Who killed you, turkey?" he asked.

The turkey said, "You did, Mr. Bergen."

Bergen turned to Mrs. B. and shrugged.

(Come to think of it, is anything in show business more absurd than starring a *ventriloquist* on radio? As well star a mime, like Marcel Marceau, or put Pavarotti in a silent picture. The public was asked to perform an act of extraordinary faith—i.e., to believe that Charlie McCarthy was actually a dummy, and that Bergen alone was talking for them both. The public consented gladly, and the act was a smash success. I wish we had it back again!)

The captain of the Princeton ice hockey team in 1925 was "Buzz" Stout, a big, good-looking youth for whom the girls fell in wriggling, giggling, lovelorn heaps. One such maiden wrote him a letter, which he showed me:

"Dearest, darling Buzz, All I want to be is a little minow [sic] frozen in the ice you skate over...."

The most difficult and dangerous steeplechase in the world is the Grand National, run at Aintree, Liverpool. The Earl of Minto rode in it five times and survived a broken neck.

Golf Nostalgia

Hickory shafts ... Baby Dimple, Penfold and Acushnet balls ... the brassie, spoon, driving iron, midiron, cleek and baffy; the jigger, mashie, wedge, and the rib-faced niblick ... the tee box full of damp sand ... the stymie ... "Emperor" Jones ... Scottish professionals ... Sarazen's plus-fours ... and his double-eagle on the 485-yard, par 5, fifteenth hole at the Augusta National in the 1935 Masters—certainly one of the most miraculous shots in the annals of the game.

When the Germans evacuated Biarritz at the end of World War II, the two blockhouses they had built on the golf links proved too massive to be either torn down or blown up, so the club turfed them over and converted them to tees. Visitors are requested to withhold facetious remarks about "shots."

There are no golf courses in Russia. I imagine it's because the people's life is hard enough without them.

Ice boats have been clocked at a speed of 120 mph.

Nor did we confine ourselves, while at the seashore, merely to terrestrial amusement, and we would frequently indulge ... in the enjoyable practice of pedal immersion. Wholly precluded for constitutional reasons from the fuller development of the art involved in swimming, we nevertheless found this to be a most laughable and even exciting occupation; and I can recall at least two occasions when, owing to a momentary inadvertence, our rolled-up trousers became partially submerged. A smart run home, however, a cup of hot milk, and immediate retirement to bed sufficed, in both instances, to protect us from any untoward results.

Augustus Carp, Esq. by Himself

Jews, saints, and Red Sox fans understand one another. They all know how to suffer.

PETER KREEFT,
A Turn of the Clock

I've been shooting doves—shooting *at* them—for more than fifty years, and I still haven't met half a dozen men who would confidently back themselves to kill the next bird over with their first barrel. I saw one excellent shot kill eleven birds with his first eleven shells, but not be able to limit out (the limit was twelve) until he reached the last (twenty-fifth) shell in his box. On the other hand, I once saw a man in Thomasville, Georgia, kill seventy-three doves with seventy-five shells. He was a mean, no-good scoundrel; we thought no more of him than he thought of observing the legal limit; but Lord, could he shoot!

Lee Trevino was asked what it was best to do if overtaken by a thunderstorm on a golf course.

"Stand in the middle of a fairway and hold up a one-iron," he said. "Not even God can hit a one-iron."

The Duke of Windsor, a mediocre golfer at best, was prouder of having scored three holes-in-one than of anything else in his life. Art Wall scored thirty-five in his professional career. But Ben Hogan, high among the titans of the game, never scored a single one.

They are not such rarities as you may think: In 1986 some 42,048 holes-in one were reported to the *Golf Digest* Holes-in-One Clearinghouse, and nobody knows how many more were scored but not reported.

Football Nostalgia

Drop kick ... nose-guards and shin-guards ... the Statue of Liberty play ... the Four Horsemen ... center rush ... moleskins and hip-pads ... the flying wedge ... the Galloping Ghost ... Walter Camp's All American teams ... the wrong-way touchdown ... halfbacks and fullbacks ...

Vice Adm. Marc A. Mitscher, who commanded the Fast Carrier Task Force in 1944, was a small, quiet man with a passion for fly fishing. One afternoon when his flagship, the carrier *Lexington*, had retired from the combat zone for refueling, he was perched in his chair on flag bridge, enjoying the sunshine and the respite. Someone mentioned fly fishing, and the admiral was off.

"I was just remembering my last day on the Miramichi," he said. "We'd fished all day without even a strike. I was tired, and dusk was falling, so I told the Indian who was handling the canoe, 'That's enough. We'll go in now.'

"The Indian said, 'No. We fish ten minutes more.'"

The admiral fell silent. We were wondering why he had told this pointless story when his soft voice resumed. "You know, I don't like being contradicted." Another pause. Then, "Especially afloat."

Eddie Eagan is the only athlete to win a gold medal in both the summer and winter Olympics. He won the light-heavyweight title at Antwerp in 1920, and was a member of the championship four-man bobsled team at Lake Placid in 1932.

The balls used in "class" sports (golf, lawn tennis, court tennis, squash, polo, etc.) are generally smaller than those in others (football, soccer, volleyball, water polo).

PAUL FUSSELL, *Class*

What football team has played the most games in the Rose Bowl?
Answer: Pasadena City College. It's their bowl.

N.H.

Baseball Nostalgia

The Sultan of Swat . . . the bottle bat . . . the Big Train . . . "Slide, Kelly, slide" . . . Joltin' Joe . . . the Splendid Splinter . . . the Meal Ticket . . . the rabbit ball . . . Connie Mack . . . Shoeless Joe ("Say it ain't so, Joe!") . . . the Georgia Peach . . . Mudville . . . the Dutchman . . . the balloon ball . . . Christy Matthewson's "fadeaway" . . . Murderer's Row . . . Tris . . . the Rabbit . . . "Buy me some peanuts and Crackerjack" . . .

The strand of rubber that wraps the core of a golf ball is about 90 feet long, when limp and unstretched. In the wrapping, it stretches to about 810 feet.

The familiar emblem on the shirts and other garments marketed by the great French tennis player René Lacoste is not an alligator, as many think, but a crocodile. When Lacoste was at the peak of his game and fame, in the 1920s, a French sportswriter nicknamed him *le Crocodile*, partly because of his saurian profile, and partly because of his ruthlessness on the tennis court, where—we should remember—he won two British titles, three French, and two U.S., plus this accolade from Bill Tilden: "René is one of the finest tennis players and tennis brains I've ever encountered." He designed a new tennis racket some years ago and is now working on a new set of golf clubs.

The morose owner [of a baseball team] once said, "Fans like to see home runs, and we have assembled a pitching staff to please our fans."

GEORGE F. WILL

One of the most spectacular finishes in the annals of golf took place a few years ago at Cypress Point, California. The star was Howard Clark of New York, playing to a handicap of four. His four-ball match was all even when they came to the fifteenth hole, 135 yards, par 3. Clark hit a short iron onto the green and sank his putt for a birdie 2. The sixteenth is 235 yards, another par 3; again Clark hit the green and sank his putt for a birdie 2. The seventeenth is the hole that professionals most admire: 375 yards, par 4, with a dog-leg across a chasm. Clark's second shot was on the green, but his putt rimmed the cup and jumped out, for a par 4. On the final hole, 350 yards, par 4, Clark's second shot hit the stick and dropped into the cup for an eagle 2—and an incredible four-hole total of 10.

Tooth and Nail

IF YOU PUT DOWN some oddments about teeth, you're almost obliged to follow with some about nails. The trouble is, I couldn't think of any, and I couldn't turn up any. Nothing in my books of quotations, nothing in Shakespeare, and only two mentions in the *Bible*: "She shall shave her head and pare her nails" (Deuteronomy 21:12); and when Nebuchadnessar went mad, "his nails were like birds' claws" (Daniel 4:33).

A dermatologist friend of mine, Dr. Tom Murrell, came to my rescue. Not all the items he gave me will make you whistle with astonishment, but at least they'll make you say, "I certainly didn't know *that*!" For instance, different nails on the same hand or foot grow at different rates. It's a fact, but there seems to be no explanation. The rate for fingernails, by the way, is about 1/32nd of an inch per week. Nails grow faster in summer than in winter, and fastest on someone between twenty years old and forty. A young man's body will replace a lost fingernail in about

116 days, but it takes close to 150 days for someone of middle age. A toenail takes about three times as long.

A fingernail may grow to five inches before it crumbles or breaks off, and a toenail to slightly shorter than that. According to the *Guinness Book of Records*, a man grew the nails on his left hand to a *total* length of 92½ inches—an average of 18½ inches per nail. His thumbnail was the longest: 23 inches. Even so, this wasn't the world's record. A man in India, presumably with time and nothing else on his hands, and nothing better to do, grew a thumbnail to 25½ inches.

The stone-faced farmer in Grant Wood's famous painting "American Gothic" was the artist's dentist.

Aged cheddar, Swiss, Monterey Jack, and certain other cheeses have been found to help prevent tooth decay.

Johnny Carson cited a report that a number of dentists were closing their offices for lack of business, and commented, "A news item like this hasn't made me so happy since I read that the Gestapo had disbanded." An irate fang-mechanic promptly sued Carson and NBC for $1 million. Quite as promptly, a judge dismissed the suit.

Until fairly recently, dentures were popular wedding gifts in the British Isles. Many people expected to lose all their teeth, and eventually did so.

Dental researchers have developed a mechanical mouth that, by taking four bites a second, can duplicate in twenty-four hours the effects of a year's chewing, and thereby speeds up the testing of dental materials.

Be true to your teeth, or they'll be false to you.

Dentist's maxim

How sharper than a serpent, to have a toothless child.

Venerable and anonymous

In Lignite, ND, it's against the law for a dentist to toss an old shoe at any woman who comes in for an appointment with her hair in rollers. In Blue Earth, MN, a law prohibits dentists from playing checkers during lunch hours. In Hosmer, IL, on the other hand, only licensed dentists are legally allowed to carry a slingshot.

American Dental Association Update News

A dentist is a cross between a watchmaker and a veterinarian.

ST. G. B.

A complete set of 32 teeth includes four kinds, each designed for a special task:

The incisors have sharp, chisel-shaped edges for biting and cutting. Four stand in the middle of each jaw.

The four canines, or "dog teeth," have jagged edges for tearing or shredding. They stand next to the incisors.

Next come the eight premolars, or bicuspids. They are double-pointed teeth, which both shred and grind.

Finally, at the ends of each arch stand the molars, 12 in all, including the wisdom teeth. The molars have flattened crowns for grinding and crushing.

A. LEOKUM

What have the following in common? Zane Gray, Doc Holliday, Paul Revere, Gen. Sir Bernard Freyberg, V.C.? Answer: Early in his career, each practiced dentistry. Zane Gray practiced in New York City until 1912, when he became an instant success as a novelist with *Riders of the Purple Sage*. Doc Holliday studied dentistry in Baltimore, at a school that later became part of the University of Maryland. From there he went west to Tombstone, Arizona, where he became a gambler and a drunkard and took part in the shoot-out at the OK corral on October 26, 1881. Paul Revere was not only a dentist, but a silversmith and engraver, a militia officer, a coroner, a poet, a health official, and the founder of Revere Copper and a successful insurance company. General Freyberg commanded the New Zealand forces in World War II.

Tooth and Nail

A prayer preceded by the use of a toothpick is of more worth than seventy-five common prayers.

MOHAMMED

Better is he who whitens a fellow man's teeth than he who gives him milk to drink.

RABBI JOHANAN

An eighteenth-century English surgeon, John Hunter, believed that human teeth could be transplanted and replanted. One of his experiments involved transplanting a healthy human tooth in a cock's comb. When the cock was killed some months later, the tooth was found to be attached.

There are many myths about George Washington's dentures. One says that he had a set of wooden teeth. He did not. But he did have teeth made of teeth and tusks from elephants, hippopotami, walruses, cattle, and humans. He was ashamed of his false teeth, and once paid his dentist to conceal his dental bills.

REIDER F. SOGNNAES, "America's Most Famous Teeth," *Smithsonian*, February 1973

Second only to the common cold, the widest-spread affliction of the human race is tooth decay. At least 90 percent of Americans are believed to suffer from it.

An old wives' tale has it that a woman loses a tooth for every child she bears.

Two false-tooth factories in Liechtenstein specialize in dark brown shades, for export to India and other countries where the people chew betel nut.

Queen Elizabeth I and Empress Josephine had such bad teeth that neither would have her portrait painted smiling.

Do not let your nails project, and keep them free of dirt.

OVID, *Ars Amatoria*

255

A toothache once beset me in Istanbul. A local friend recommended his dentist, so I went to consult him. A sign on the door at his address directed me upstairs, to:

Dr. Mohammed Ali, D.D.S.
2th Floor

Tributes
(CONT'D)

In 1916, when Lt. Col. Johnson Hagood was serving at Fort Douglas, Utah, he was required to prepare an efficiency report on a junior officer, Capt. George C. Marshall. In answer to the question, "Would you desire to have this officer under your immediate command?" Hagood wrote, "Yes, but I would prefer to serve *under his command*." (Hagood's italics)

In late 1943–44, I was a lieutenant, U.S.N.R., on duty with the Fighter Command South Pacific Forces, at Munda in the Solomons. The commanders and their assistants met every morning at 6:30 for reports and discussions. We were about twenty-five altogether, usually including several high-brass visitors. I was a few minutes late one morning; the meeting had already started. I took a seat in the back of the tent, and was half-listening to the aerology officer's invariable prediction—"In the afternoon, scattered thunder-showers over the land area"—

when I suddenly had a strange, strong awareness that I was in the presence, even the proximity, of greatness. An extraordinarily powerful personality was in that tent.

I looked around. I could see only the backs of the heads of the officers up front, and they told me nothing. When the meeting broke up, I stood aside and watched. There he came, and as he passed me, I felt my scalp tingle with the electricity of his aura. It was General Marshall, chief of staff of the U.S. Army. I had never seen him before and I never saw him again, but one lowly serviceman will never forget him.

Toward the end of the second World War, two sailors were walking along a passageway in Admiral Halsey's flagship, the U.S.S. *Missouri*. One said, "Halsey? I'd go through hell for that old son of a bitch!"

A finger like a marlinspike jabbed him between the shoulderblades, and a gruff voice said, "Young man, I'm not so old!"

> FLEET ADM. WILLIAM F. HALSEY and
> J. BRYAN, III, *The Halsey Story*

Admiral Halsey was attending a reception in 1946 when a woman broke through the crowd around him, grasped his hand, and cried, "I feel as if I were touching the hand of God!" Halsey turned to his flag lieutenant; "Did you hear that idiot? For sixty-three years I've been plain 'Bill Halsey,' and now I'm suddenly God! It'll take some getting used to."

Mendelssohn said of Jenny Lind, "As great an artist as ever lived, and the greatest I have known." And Chopin said of her, "Her singing is pure and true; the charm of her soft passages is beyond description." (But see The Cruel Critics, pages 55–58). When she dropped one of her gloves on the way to her first concert in New York City, in 1821, a bystander rushed to pick it up and at once began charging a shilling for the privilege of kissing it.

The London stage of the twenties and thirties found a goddess in Tallulah Bankhead. No debutante ever swept into Mayfair with such gaiety and success. . . . Her admirers in churches and places where they sing, substituted Tallulah for Alleluia and it sounded charming on the organ—Talleluia!

SHANE LESLIE, *Long Shadows*

When P. G. Wodehouse was made a Doctor of Philosophy at Oxford, the Public Orator acclaimed him as *"lepidissimus, facetissimus, venustissimus, iocosissimus, ridibundissimus"*—i.e., a very funny fellow.

I played Ophelia in John Gielgud's Hamlet on Broadway in 1936, a most remarkable experience. He didn't *play* Hamlet, he *was* Hamlet. It was the only play I was ever in when stagehands stood in the wings to watch.

LILLIAN GISH

John Steinbeck: "Fred Allen is unquestionably our best humorist, a brilliant critic of manners and morals." Herman Wouk: "Fred Allen is America's greatest satiric wit in our time." James Thurber: "You can count on the thumb of one hand that American who is at once a comedian, a humorist, a wit, and a satirist, and his name is Fred Allen."

Miss Lizzie Van Lew, known as "Richmond's beautiful Yankee spy," is buried there under a boulder from Beacon Hill in Boston. Its inscription reads,

> SHE RISKED EVERYTHING THAT IS DEAR TO MAN
> FRIENDS—FORTUNE—COMFORT—HEALTH—LIFE ITSELF
> ALL FOR THE ONE ABSORBING DESIRE OF HER HEART—
> THAT SLAVERY MIGHT BE ABOLISHED
> AND THE UNION PRESERVED

I have resisted the temptation to include Senator Vest's "Tribute to the Dog."

Typos and Blemishes

(CONT'D)

WHEN J. C. SQUIRE was writing for *The New Statesman* about Shakespeare's plays, he found that Hermia (in *A Midsummer Night's Dream*) appeared as "Hernia" in his proof. He let it stand, with an asterisk, indicating an author's note. In it he said, "I cannot bring myself to interfere with my printer's first fine careless rupture."

IVOR BROWN,
A Charm of Names

I didn't see this one myself, and I doubt that it ever occurred, but I'm told that the New York *Daily News* ran a photo of the late Mr. Onassis making a tour of Buster Keaton's house in Hollywood. The caption read,

ARISTOTLE CONTEMPLATING
THE HOME OF BUSTER

260

A splendidly ambiguous headline introduced a story on the front page of the Chicago *Journal* when I worked there in the late 1920s. Does anyone now remember the Dolly Gann controversy? I do, but largely because of the headline. To recap it, Vice President Charles Curtis, a bachelor, had asked his sister, Dolly Gann, to act as his official hostess. The question was, did she take precedence over the wife of a certain other high government official? Secretary of State Henry Lewis Stimson ruled that she did not, and the V.P. protested, as follows, according to the *Journal*:

CURTIS REQUESTS STIMSON TO
REVERSE HIMSELF ON HIS SISTER

If I may be permitted another bit of bawdry, this one comes from a Bombay paper and concerns the Chappaquiddick tragedy. The paper intended to explain that it had occurred after an informal American party called a "cook out," but there was a vital misprint in the first word.

The head that every desk man dreams of writing:

POPE ELOPES

Here are a few beauties collected and published by the *Columbia Journalism Review*:

ROCK STAR HIT WITH SICK CHILD
Mansfield, O., *News*

FUEL FOR CITY BUSES PASSES THROUGH TWO MIDDLEMEN
Detroit Free Press

IDAHO GROUP ORGANIZES TO HELP SERVICE WIDOWS
Idaho Statesman

EXPLODING COMMODE FLOODS POLAND
[Poland is the name of a dormitory.]
College Heights Herald
Bowling Green, Ky.

MAN MINUS EAR WAIVES HEARING
Jackson, Tenn., *Sun*

HIS BURNING REAR END IS A MAJOR DISTRACTION
Toronto *Star*

JERK INJURES NECK, WINS AWARD
Buffalo *News*

RHODE ISLAND SECRETARY EXCITES FURNITURE EXPERTS
Newark *Star-Ledger*

KICKING BABY CONSIDERED TO BE HEALTHY
Burlington *Free Press*

SEASON OFFERS RARE OPPORTUNITY TO GOOSE HUNTERS
San Diego *Union*

The sedate old *Saturday Evening Post* of fifty-odd years ago ran an article by the wife of a billiards professional in which she told how part of her job as his assistant was seeing that all was in order for his exhibitions. For instance, she had to make sure that the billiard balls were exactly at room temperature. The *Post*'s make-up editor decided that a subhead was needed here, so he wrote it:

SHE KEEPS HIS BALLS WARM

Nearly a million copies had gone out before someone woke up.

Understatements

ADM. SIR JOHN FISHER [the First Sea Lord] demonstrated his faith in the submarine by taking the Prince [later King George V] to sea in one of them off Portsmouth. Princess Mary [later Queen Mary], who remained on the quay, was heard to murmur, "I shall be very disappointed if George does not come up again."

KENNETH ROSE, King George V

When the space shuttle exploded over Cape Canaveral in 1985, killing the seven astronauts aboard, NASA's TV commentator remarked, "There appears to have been a major malfunction."

And Bill Sims says that when he was an air-raid warden in London during World War II, all such disasters as the total destruction of a house by a 500-pound bomb were reported under "Incidents."

Understatements

I understand that the Sahara has a very light soil.

A British MP

Russ Forgan told me that when he was chairman of the Senior Council at Princeton, Class of 1922, the college proctors brought in two grinning young sophomores and read off a list of charges that made even the hardened Council wince and whistle. It began with entertaining known prostitutes in the dormitory, possession of alcohol, drunkenness, rowdiness and general nudity, and ran through such catch-alls as "disorderly conduct, disturbing the peace, creating a nuisance," and other offenses of the same disgraceful, reprehensible ilk.

The miscreants didn't seem at all contrite; instead, they giggled and preened themselves. Seeing this, Russ put on his sternest face and announced that though it was within the Council's power to have them beheaded for such unparalleled depravity, he himself was inclined toward clemency, and might merely sentence them to life on Devil's Island if they could produce even one mitigating circumstance. "What have you to say for yourselves, gentlemen?"

They whispered together for a moment. Then the spokesman said, "Well, sirs, there's this: Our little party wasn't at all *formal*, you understand. It was just plain, innocent heigh-ho."

Dr. Guillotin ... had perfected his celebrated machine by 1791. The conception was humanitarian; the condemned person, he said, addressing the assembled legislators of revolutionary France, would feel only "*a slight freshness on the neck.*"

PETER QUENNELL,
"Civil Service"

"Tain't nuttin' I'd run uphill on a hot day to do."

Vermont saying

NAVY FAULTS PILOT'S JUDGMENT
IN DOWNING ANOTHER U.S. JET
Maine Sunday Telegram

Vanity
(CONT'D)

THEY TALK, SAYS SHERIDAN, of avarice, lust, ambition, as great passions. It is a mistake; they are little passions. Vanity is the great commanding passion of all. It is this that produces the most grand and heroic deeds, or impels to the most dreadful crimes. Save me from this passion, and I can defy the others. They are mere urchins, but this is a giant.

TOM MOORE, *Journal*

Admiral Nelson's death at Trafalgar was due directly to his vanity or, if you prefer, to his insistence on wearing a costume appropriate to the occasion. Whatever his motive, his full-dress uniform, with its stars and medals and ribbons, signified his importance for the sharpshooter perched aloft in an enemy ship. (Nelson's uniform, and the musket ball that killed him, are on view in the Lloyds Insurance Building in London.)

Vanity

Ina Claire, the famous and accomplished stage star, married John Gilbert, the romantic hero of the silent screen. The advent of talking pictures doomed his career (and the marriage), because of his high, squeaky voice. But while things were still rosy, a reporter accosted the couple in a restaurant and asked Miss Claire how it felt to be married to a celebrity.

She said, "Why don't you ask my husband?"

> Full of mine own soul, perfect of myself,
> Towards mine and me sufficient.
>
> ALGERNON SWINBURNE, "Althea"

[The English painter] Charles Jervas (1675–1749), having succeeded happily in copying (in *surpassing*, he thought) a picture of Titian's, looked first at one, then at the other, and then with parental complacency cried, "Poor little Tit! How he would stare!"

HORACE WALPOLE

Verses

(CONT'D)

I always utter a little glad cry
When a rose in a garden I espy;
    It's the only flower I'm sure about,
    Beyond the shadow of a doubt.

DR. W. E. FARBSTEIN

The dreariest sound in the world
    Is a freight train whistle at night,
And the next most dreary sound
    Is a husband saying, "Aaaaal-l-l-right!"
        In the bored, exhausted, worn-out tone
        That means "I want to be let alone."

IB.

I think of when I was brash and rash,
    When the bloom of my youth had dew on it,
And I'm very grateful life didn't cash
    Every check that I drew on it.

IB.

Two limericks

There was a Buff Orpington hen
Who dined with a goose and a wren.
　"Bless, O Lord," said the goose,
　"This food to our use,
And ourselves to Thy service. Amen!"

and

An epicure dining at Crewe
Found quite a large mouse in his stew.
　Cried his waiter, "Don't shout
　And wave it about,
Or the rest will be wanting one too!"

There is a flower that blooms so bright,
　Some call it marigold-a,
And he that wold not when he might,
　May not when he wold-a.

269

A sheep and a goat were walking through a pasture.
 Said the sheep to the goat, "Can you walk a little faster?"
  Said the goat to the sheep, "My toe is so'."
  "Excuse me, goat! I did not know."

As I was laying on the green,
A small English book I seen.
Carlyle's *Essay on Burns* was the edition,
So I left it laying in the same position.

Anon.

Standin on de corner, doin' no harm,
'Long come a 'leeceman, cotch me by de arm.
'Leeceman, 'leeceman, tarn me loose!
I wanna go home to de buzzards' roos'!

POLK MILLER

Nonsense Latin popular with schoolboys:

Isabile haeres ego
Fortibuses in aro.
O nobile themistrux
Vatiscenum pes andux.

Ef you don' lak mah peaches,
 Don' you shake on mah tree,
'Cause Ah's a freestone peach—
 Don' nothin' cling around me!
Oh, baby, how long has Ah got to wait?
Kin Ah git you now, or mus' Ah hesi-ma-tate?
(You got to hesi-ma-tate!)

"The Stable-boy's Song"

The Very Rich
(CONT'D)

A Texan came to New York to discuss investments with his broker. The broker valued him as a customer and gave a dinner party in his honor. Seated next to him was a patronizing woman who opened the conversation with "I'm told you're from Texas. So I suppose you have a ten-thousand-acre ranch, like all Texans?"

"No'm," he said. "Nothin' like that. Mine's just an itty-bitty place."

"How big is 'itty-bitty'?"

"Three acres, ma'am."

"Mercy! What do you call it, Kozy Korner?"

"No'm, most folks call it Downtown Dallas."

"A man with a million dollars can be as happy nowadays as though he were rich."

WARD MCALLISTER

The writer remembers meeting a certain Indian potentate at a luncheon party. The host said to him: "May I ask why you commanded your new fleet of Rolls-Royces built with such high roofs?" The maharajah replied, "Oh, I don't know. I might want to wear an aigrette."

SACHEVERELL SITWELL,
Portugal and Madeira

And a man in Sewickley, Pennsylvania, instructed his valet to shine the soles of his shoes, "In case I might wish to cross my legs."

Among the steady customers of the Remington Hotel in Houston is the lady who comes in once a week for a breakfast of deep-fried potato skins, a glass of milk, and an eight-ounce can of caviar. Her breakfast check is approximately $650.

C. D. B. BRYAN in *Esquire*

The *Daily Telegraph* had a picture of the richest man in the world—capital $700 million. A face with *no* expression except gloom, worry, and dyspepsia. Bankrupts invariably look plump, hilarious, and obviously without a care in the world.

GEORGE LYTTELTON

Sir Kenneth Clark, director of the British Museum, wrote an entertaining autobiography, *Another Part of the Wood*. Among his anecdotes is one about his father's new yacht, a huge one. He took delivery at Mentone, and three days later in his pride and delight, he gave a luncheon party. Here I turn the story over to Sir Kenneth:

Amongst the guests was Madame Herriot, proprietress of a store named the Louvre, then the most prosperous in Paris. "It is delightful," she said to my father. "I would give *anything* for a yacht like this."

"Anything?"

"Yes, anything."

My father named an enormous sum.

"But it must include everything."

"Yes, everything."

"Even the notepaper."

"Yes, the notepaper."

"And I must have it tomorrow."

"Yes, tomorrow."

Accommodation was found in neighbouring hotels, we all packed hastily, and Madame Herriot came on board next morning with her cheque.

The wife of William Morris, later Lord Niffield, applied for membership in the smart Huntercombe golf club. She was refused because of a rule that admitted the families of gentlemen only; whereupon Morris bought up the whole place, presenting it to his wife on her birthday.

ELIZABETH LONGFORD,
Condensed from *The Pebbled Shore*

When Mrs. Jack Gardner of Boston learned that Mr. Potter Palmer of Chicago had a gold table service for fifty settings, she asked in pretty innocence, "But what does Mrs. Palmer do when she has company?"

LUCIUS BEEBE, *The Big Spenders*

James Gordon Bennett's [yacht] *Namouna* carried a cow housed on its foredeck, against the unlikely contingency of its owner's wanting milk.

I.B.

No rich man is ugly.

ZSA-ZSA GABOR

Money isn't everything, but it's the best way to keep score.

RALPH WHEELER,
Tulsa, Oklahoma

A young man seeing Aristotle Onassis for the first time remarked to his companion, "He's not very tall, is he?"

"Maybe not," she said, "but when he stands on his money, he's the tallest man in the room."

Veronica Wedge was one of those girls who, if they have not plenty of precious stones on their persons, feel nude.

P. G. WODEHOUSE,
Galahad at Blandings

According to Hy Gardner's column, the personal expenses of Adam Khashoggi, the Saudi Arabian oil billionaire, are $353,000 a day.

W. Alton Jones, chairman of the executive committee of Cities Service, was killed in an airplane crash in 1962. He was known to enjoy carrying large sums of money, so when his body was recovered from the wreckage, the searchers were not surprised to find in his pockets $7,000 in traveler's checks and $55,690 in cash, including one $10,000 bill.

The wretchedness of being rich is that you have to live with rich people.

LOGAN PEARSALL SMITH

John D. Rockefeller always sees a little farther than the rest of us—and then he sees around the corner.

JOHN D. ARCHBOLD,
Rockefeller's partner in Standard Oil

[In Delhi, Shah Jeaan] spent his days in a pool containing forty niches in which he and thirty-nine wives sat neck-deep in warm water while over them were sprayed forty different scents, one for each; between their feet swam a glittering variety of oriental fish with jewels round their necks and tails, while into his hand was pressed a goblet cut from a single ruby. Sparkling waterfalls—iridescent from various colored lights placed behind them—rested their vision until dark, when boats of silver and golden hue conveyed them to love trysts in pagodas again surrounded by the eternal scented waters.

SIR OSWALD MOSLEY,
My Life

If you want to know what God thinks of money, you have only to look at some of the people he gives it to.

Anon.

A million dollars doesn't sound like a lot, if you say it fast.

RICK GRAY, a Dallas
real-estate developer

In 1939, a Dutch baron hired a locomotive and tender at Deauville and took the Casino orchestra to Paris and back (about 250 miles round trip), playing full blast the whole way.

John D. Rockefeller, Jr.,'s second wife was some years younger than he. Someone sneered, "What did he give her for a wedding present? Blocks?"
"Yes, the blocks between Fifth and Sixth avenues, and Forty-Eighth and Fifty-Second streets."

When you visit the S. family's granite castle, the paper napkin you are given at your first meal will be yours for all subsequent meals.

To celebrate the lifting of the siege of Gibraltar (1782–86), the British Commander-in-Chief in Ireland gave a dinner in honor of the Lord Lieutenant. The feature of the dessert course was a representation of the fortress, executed in confectionery.

275

It was a faithful portrayal of the Rock, together with the works, batteries, and artillery of the besiegers, which threw sugar plums against the walls. The expense of this ostentatious piece of magnificence did not fall short of £1500.

LUCIUS BEEBE,
The Big Spenders

Voices
(CONT'D)

He has a voice that sounds as if it were coming up an elevator shaft.

GEORGE ADE

"What a crumbly yellow voice you have," said S, the Russian mnemonist (see page 154) to the psychologist who was examining him.

Stout-hearted Stentor, whose great brazen voice has all the volume of fifty men shouting.

Iliad, Book V

The Museum of the Spoken Word, in Brussels, has more than 5,000 recordings of famous voices, including Lenin's, Jean Cocteau's, James Joyce's, and Ogden Nash's.

A voice like a soprano hyena.

LAWTON MACKALL

Shelley's voice was not only dissonant, like a jarring string, but he spoke in sharp fourths, the most unpleasant sequence of sounds that can fall on the human ear.

THOMAS LOVE PEACOCK

(Peacock should know; a peacock's voice is surely the most exacerbating in the animal kingdom.)

Fred Allen's voice sounds like a man with false teeth chewing on slate pencils.

O. O. MCINTYRE

H. G. Wells and Arnold Bennett had squeaky voices, and Bismarck's was almost a falsetto.

Keats describes the sharp voices of his friend Brown's nephews as "little voices, like wasp stings."

The University Bookman

When many foreigners, especially the English, sneer at American voices as "nasal," what they mean is the Yankee twang, for the native voices of the Middle Atlantic States are soft and pleasant. Moreover, "nasal" is the wrong word for what those foreigners mean, as you can prove by pinching your nostrils together when you speak. Your voice does *not* come through your nose, and therefore is not nasal.

Wants

(CONT'D)

ONE OF MY WANTS is more of those lusty old folk ballads of seventy-five or a hundred years ago, like "Steamboat Bill," "The Wreck of Old '97," "The Sinking of the *Titanic*," "Jesse James," "The Death of William Jennings Bryan," "Casey Jones," and such.

This particular half-dozen are solemn, not to say lugubrious. But plenty of others are—well, *rollicking*. "The Bastard King of England," for instance, "Christopher Columbo," "The Harlot of Jerusalem," "Lydia Pinkham," "The Beta Song," "The Scotch Tattooed La-dee" (or is she Swiss?), and—probably the best known of the lot—"Frankie and Johnny."

On second thought, "rollicking" isn't strong enough; the few staves that I retain are so downright bawdy that they are fit—in H. L. Mencken's description of similar stuff—"only for audiences of policemen, newspaper reporters and medical students." Still, even a professional bluenose would have a hard time choking back a belly-laugh at some of the flights of fancy—which

279

raises the question: Why does nobody write them any more? It can't be for a lack of subjects! My ears tingle and my mouth waters when I consider what a good, gittar-strummin' country balladeer could do with "The Bridge at Chappy-quiddick."

A way to tell when a melon is at its peak of ripeness without cutting into it.

Elimination of the "blind spot" to the left rear of your automobile.

I'd also welcome a good comedy series along the line of Fred Allen's, Jack Benny's, Rowan and Martin's, even Milton Berle's, with a cast of characters whom we would come to know and enjoy (Rochester, the Judge, Titus Moody, Charlie McCarthy, Falstaff Openshaw) and absurd, running catch-lines ("Vas you dere, Sharlie?" ... "It's a joke, son!" ... "Wanna buy a duck?" ... "Beautiful downtown Burbank" ... "Howdy, bub!" and so on).

Please, some comedian, come through and fast!

A fail-safe tactic for use when propositioning your date.

An instant cure for hiccoughs.

A way to stop a jingle or catch phrase from running around in your head.

A "want" that must surely be unique was declared to my grandfather by one of the family servants, Unc' Jack Tazewell (pronounced "Tazz'l"). Grandfather asked him what he would choose if Divine Providence offered to grant him one wish. Unc' Jack answered, "A eye on de en' o' my fingah, so's Ah could s'arch de back o' mah haid."

I'd like to know whatever became of some of my treasures that were lost or stolen.

Weather

IF SOMEONE TELLS YOU, "The temperature was forty below zero," you don't need to ask, "Fahrenheit or Centigrade?" They are exactly the same at that point—and that one alone.

Ellen Glasgow, the Virginia novelist, said, "If I have one gift, it's for bringing unprecedented weather with me, wherever I go."

The average January temperatures in the Scandinavian countries are warmer than you probably realize. In Helsinki, it's 23 degrees Fahrenheit, Oslo, 25 degrees, Stockholm, 27 degrees, Copenhagen and Reykjavik, 32 degrees. The January average in Minneapolis is 12 degrees and in Duluth, 9 degrees.

At Silver Lake, Colorado, on April 14–15, 1921, 76 inches of snow fell.

Thank heavens, the sun has gone in, and I don't have to go out and enjoy it.

LOGAN PEARSALL SMITH

A lady was importuning Sheridan the playwright to take a walk with her. "Look, the weather has cleared up enough."

"Perhaps enough for one," Sheridan said, "but not for two."

To go to St. Paul's Cathedral [in winter] is certain death. The thermometer is several degrees below zero. My sentences are frozen as they come out of my mouth, and are thawed in the course of the summer, making strange noises and unexpected assertions in various parts of the church.

SYDNEY SMITH

One very foggy dark morning, I said to Alfred [his manservant], "What have you done to make such a morning as this?"

He said, "It isn't morning, Sir. It's only what's left over from yesterday."

SAMUEL BUTLER, *On Alfred*

I have been refreshing myself with a walk in the garden, where I find that January (who according to Chaucer was the husband of May) being dead, February had married the widow.

WILLIAM COWPER, *Letters*

283

The English winter: ending in July to recommence in August.

LORD BYRON

At the South Pole weather station on the evening of September 17, 1957, the thermometer registered $-102.1°F.$, the lowest official reading ever recorded.

National Geographic

Weddings

A COUSIN OF MINE said this happened at an afternoon wedding in St. Paul's Church, Richmond. Her uncle, an elderly and distinguished judge, was shown to a pew in front of her, where, to her amazement, he opened a newspaper. She tapped his shoulder and whispered, "Uncle Dan, you really shouldn't read a newspaper at a wedding."

The judge said mildly, "My dear child, I've seen a thousand weddings, but I haven't seen this afternoon's paper"—and went on reading.

No matter what sort of show Fannie Brice was in, she insisted that there be a part for Roger Davis, even if only a walk-on. He wasn't a good actor and he didn't have much stage presence, but she liked to have him around because he was so funny. Weddings always make me think of Roger. The last time I saw him was at a wedding in St. Bartholomew's in New York. He and I were among the dozen ushers, and I remember my astonishment and delight when Roger, escorting two elderly ladies up the aisle, stopped beside one of the marble pillars and instantly became a typical Roman guide, thus:

"Deece de oldes' churrrrrch in Rome," he intoned. "Deece column sol-leed olla-boster. Hold a match on t'other side, lakness of de Saviorrrr appearce on deece side. Follow me, pleece!"

The ladies must have felt that they had wandered Through the Looking Glass, but they followed him.

This was the same wedding at which another of the ushers whispered to me, "Stick with me after the ceremony! I know a short cut through the vestry to the bar in the Waldorf."

Dick K. heard this at a wedding on Long Island:

The clergyman pronounced them man and wife, the groom kissed the bride, and a child's clear voice asked, "Mummy, is this where he sprinkles the pollen on her?"

Attila the Hun died (in 453) from a hemorrhage brought on by excessive drinking of mead (a fermented mixture of honey and water) at a wedding feast.

Jim McC. told me that when he became engaged, it fell to him to introduce his mother and his fiancée's. The meeting was not a success. The mothers-in-law-to-be took an instant and violent dislike to each other, and subsequent meetings were no more cordial. The climax came at the wedding itself, Jim said. His mother was escorted to the front pew on the right, and his fiancée's to the front pew on the left. And there, across the aisle from each other, in full view of the company assembled, the two of them fumed, cursing the couturier who had sold them identical costumes.

Early in the Episcopal marriage ceremony, the groom declares, "I take thee to my wedded wife . . . and thereto I plight thee my troth." The bride then makes the same declaration, verbatim, except for "my wedded husband" and "I give thee my troth." Why *give* instead of *plight*? What is the distinction? I hope some reader will enlighten me.

I was once in a wedding where the maid of honor accompanied the bride and groom on their honeymoon. Your surmise is right: The marriage didn't last long. I also remember a wedding reception where the happy couple drove away in a shower of rice and a whirl of ribbons; and, a few minutes later, the bride's father drove away too—and never came back.

Rosa Lewis (of the Cavendish Hotel in London) threw her wedding ring at her new husband as they came out of the church, and never spoke to him again.

Among the guests at Princess Elizabeth and Prince Philip's wedding were five kings, eight queens, ten princesses, and—by the groom's personal invitation—a bartender, Félix, from Cannes.

Unless the bride weeps at her wedding, the marriage is doomed. This superstition derives from another: that a witch is able to shed only three tears, and those from her left eye. Therefore, when a bride weeps copiously, it proves she is not a witch, and has not "plighted her troth to Satan."

An invitation to a wedding involves more trouble than a summons to a police court.

WILLIAM PALMER

The original purpose of the bride's veil was to conceal her maidenly blushes from the onlookers.

The fourth finger of the left hand ("the medical finger" to the Greeks and Romans) was designated the ring finger because of a belief that a vein ran from its tip direct to the heart.

A century or two ago, wedding rings were often inscribed with "posies" like these:

> Our contract
> Was Heaven's act
>
> In thee, my choice,
> I do rejoice

and this witty one: My love is endless as this.

Hollywood brides keep the bouquet and throw away the groom.

GROUCHO MARX

In Sweden, the wedding guests throw birdseed at the bride and groom.

There was a wedding in Cincinnati where, halfway through the ceremony, the nervous groom fainted. His ushers carried him to the vestry room and brought him around with slaps and brandy. In a few minutes, the service was able to resume. When it was over, and the bridal couple came back down the aisle, all smiles, the whole church cheered and applauded.

Some women were discussing a recent wedding. One said, "I had a very nice note from the bride, thanking me for my present, but it began in the most extraordinary way: 'Who but you'— she wrote—'would have chosen that beautiful whatever-it-was.' Who but you! Really!"

Another woman said, "That's exactly how she began her note to me: 'Who but you—' "

"And me!" said a third.

To this day the bride is privately known as "Who-but-you."

S. C. W.

I know of a Miss Sparrow who married a Mr. Hawk; and a Miss Rose Wilde who married and divorced a Mr. Bull, thereby becoming Mrs. Wilde Bull.

The bridal business runs to $27.5 billion a year.

Bride's Magazine

The same Robert Quillen who wrote and printed the birth announcement on page 27 also wrote and printed the wedding announcement that follows (slightly abridged):

The groom hasn't done a lick of work since he got shipped from college. He manages to dress well and keep a supply of spending money because his dad is a soft-hearted old fool who takes up his bad checks instead of letting him go to jail where he belongs.

The bride is a skinny, fast little idiot who has been kissed and handled by every boy in town since she was twelve years old. She paints like a Sioux Indian, sucks cigarettes and drinks mean liquor. She doesn't know how to cook, sew or keep house.

The groom wore a rented dinner suit. His patent leather shoes matched his state in tightness and harmonized with the axle-grease polish on his hair. In addition to his jag [intoxication], he carried a dun [bill] for the ring and his usual look of imbecility.

The young people will make their home with the bride's parents, which means they will sponge on the old man until he dies, and then she will take in washing. They expect a blessed event in about five months.

"The Sage of Fountain Inn," as Quillen was known, died in 1948, in his early sixties. He was not a native South Carolinian, by the way; he was born in Kansas.

It is considered the best of luck for the groom to stop on the way to his wedding and shake hands with a chimney sweep. Prince Philip, Duke of Edinburgh, did so on his way to marry Princess Elizabeth.

John Ray's *English Proverbs* (1670) says this of a lazy wife: "She broke her arm coming out of the church door and never worked again."

289

Here's another of Ray's wedding comments: "They tied a knot with their tongues that they couldn't untie with their teeth."

A press photographer told me about an evening wedding at which the bridesmaids wore strapless gowns. The bride tossed her bouquet a trifle high, and when the target bridesmaid stretched to catch it, out They popped. The bridesmaid caught the bouquet, and the photographer caught the picture.

It was a beautiful wedding. Everything went smoothly until after the "I dos," when the wedding party marched back up the aisle. The groom's grandfather had got halfway when his pants fell down. Everybody burst out laughing. He calmly bent over and pulled them up and continued walking.

A CORRESPONDENT in the
Richmond (Va.) *News Leader*

My young daughters had returned from a marriage ceremony and were playing "wedding." When the oldest, who was the minister, said, "Do you take this man for richer or poorer?" the bride replied firmly, "For richer."

JOHN DOHERTY, *The Reader's Digest*

When the wedding party is barefoot and dressed in blue jeans, and the ceremony is held out of doors, and the bride wears a wreath of wild flowers, and the musicians play only rock throughout, I give the marriage one year and not a month more.

C. J. V. MURPHY

What the bride said as she entered the church: "Aisle . . . altar . . . hymn. . . ."

JOHN R. COURNYER

Mets outfielder Mookie Wilson on why he was wed in a ball-park: "My wife wanted a big diamond."

Sports Illustrated

Weird Wagers

(CONT'D)

THOMAS WHALEY (1766–1800) was an Irish gentleman, gallant and reckless, who made no account of money, limb, or life, when a bet was to be won, or a daring deed to be attempted. . . . He rendered himself a cripple for life by jumping from the drawing-room window of Daly's clubhouse [Dublin] on to the roof of a hackney coach which was passing.

Condensed from
Buck Whaley's Memoirs

Dick Perkins told me about a bet his great-grandfather had made in London a hundred years ago: that he could drive a coach-and-four down Piccadilly. Everyone knew this was against the law, so the bet was snapped up. The day came, the coach-and-four turned into Piccadilly, and the driver was promptly arrested—and as promptly released, when he pointed out that the law specified a coach and four *horses*, whereas his hitch—as the constable could plainly see—was three horses and a mule.

Words
(CONT'D)

ACCORDING TO DOROTHY PARKER, the two most beautiful words in the English language are "Check enclosed." They may be the most beautiful *written* words, but the spoken words are "In conclusion."

The longest word in English is the chemical name for tryptophan synthetase; it contains 1,913 letters. But scientific words aside, the longest in the magisterial *Oxford English Dictionary* is floccinaucinihilipilification. You'd think it was a specimen word, kept on a shelf in a jar of formaldehyde, like a two-headed fetus, but Senator Moynihan managed to use it in a review of John Kenneth Galbraith's autobiography, *A Life in Our Times*, in *The New Yorker*. It means "the action or habit of estimating as worthless."

The difference between the right word and the almost right word is the difference between lightning and the lightning bug.

MARK TWAIN

What do these words have in common? *hijack, canopy, stupid, crabcake, first, calmness, afghan?*

Answer: Each contains three successive letters of the alphabet.

W. S. SIMS

Words short and rare

aglet: the metal tip on a shoelace.

brills: the hair on a horse's eyelids.

chert: a flintlike rock.

ers: a legume cultivated for ground cover or fodder.

fid: a wooden pin used in splicing rope.

fleer: to laugh coarsely or impudently.

geek: a carnival performer who bites the heads off live chickens or snakes.

keek: to peep.

prin: a stick with a noose for holding the nose of a refractory animal.

quark: the smallest "building block" of matter that has been so far identified.

quern: a small hand mill for grinding pepper, mustard, spices.

quop: to palpitate.

rudd: a freshwater fish.

slub: a lump on a thread; unevenness in a woven fabric.

smew: a small wild duck.

swelp: a chronic complainer (from "So help me, God.")

thode: a sudden gust of wind.

thole: to put up with.

treen: objects made of wood.

trug: a garden basket with wooden underpinnings.

FINIS

Reader, *Carthagenia* was of the mind that unto those *Three Things* which the Ancients held Impossible, there should be added this *Fourth*, to find a Book printed without *Errata*. It seems the Hands of *Briareus*, and the Eyes of *Argus* will not prevent them.

COTTON MATHER,
Magnalia Christi Americana

J. (for "Joseph") Bryan, III, was born in Richmond, Virginia, in 1904. He graduated from Princeton in 1927, traveled in Europe, Russia, Persia, India, and East Africa, and returned home, briefly, to write editorials and features for the *Richmond News Leader.* He left Richmond again in 1930 to work first on the *Chicago Journal,* then *Time, Fortune, Parade* (Cleveland), *The New Yorker, Town and Country* (as managing editor), and finally *The Saturday Evening Post* (as associate editor). He resigned from the *Post* in 1940 to become a freelance and has been one ever since. His articles have appeared in all the major American magazines, and he has written many books, including *The Windsor Story* (in collaboration with Charles J. V. Murphy), which was a main selection of the Book-of-the-Month Club, *The Sword over the Mantel,* his personal "recollections" of what he calls "the War of Northern Aggression," *Merry Gentlemen (and One Lady),* sketches of his friends Fred Allen, Robert Benchley, Dorothy Parker, and other great wits of our time; and most recently *Hodgepodge,* the forerunner of this book. After serving in the Army (1st lieutenant), Navy (lieutenant commander), and Air Force (colonel), Bryan returned to Richmond for good in 1959, and lives there in a house built by his great-great-great-grandfather.